YES!
I AM
FED UP.
NOW WHAT?

4 SELF-DRIVEN STEPS TO **MOVE**
YOUR WELL-BEING AND WORK FORWARD

BRIDGETTE L. COLLINS

Editing by The Pro Book Editor
Cover Design by MiblArt
Interior Design by IAPS.rocks
Author photo by Amanda Feliciano

eBook ISBN: 978-0-9790932-6-5
paperback ISBN: 978-0-9790932-7-2

    1. Main category—SELF-HELP/Personal Growth/Success
    2. Other category—BUSINESS & ECONOMICS/Personal Success
    3. Other category—SELF-HELP/Self-Management/General

First Edition

To all the people in the world who are not afraid to
MOVE out of their "fed-up" state of being.

Contents

SELF-NARRATION

INTRODUCTION

How many times in your life have you said to yourself, "I'm fed up with [insert the name of that someone or something]?" If you didn't use the words "fed up," maybe you said you were tired of [insert the name of that someone or something] or frustrated with [insert the name of that someone or something], which is basically the same as saying you are fed up. Whether you said you were fed up, tired, or frustrated, how many times have you asked yourself, "Now what?" Probably never because we tend to accept situations "as is" and settle on being fed up, tired, and frustrated.

If you ask others around you like I did, you'll find almost everyone has experienced some level of frustration with someone or something in their lives, such as their workplace environment, homelife, health, access to equitable healthcare, the cost of prescription drugs, the economy, the rise of crime in our neighborhoods, the lack of respect for one another in the world, the political divide, etcetera. When I think about the people and things we can get frustrated with or tired of, I refer to those stressors as "unwanted passengers." When we don't recognize life's frustrations for what they are, we can't plan past the obstacles and will find ourselves unhappily driving around with them on rough and bumpy roads for years. But you don't have to be forever burdened by unwanted passengers like marital problems, financial setbacks, health concerns, work woes, unhealthy relationships, etcetera.

Through my years as a human resources (HR) professional for state and local governmental agencies, an HR business partner for a variety of small companies, a certified personal trainer, and a certified running coach, I have witnessed countless people on their respective roads settling for unhappy and unfulfilled lives. They allow the unwanted passengers to keep them in a "fed-up" state of being. They can't dream, they can't see a different perspective, and they can't move or evolve because they're stuck on thoughts, feelings, and actions related to their unwanted passengers.

One good thing about being fed up is that it can provoke inward and outward consciousness, as well as a new attitude, perspective, and behaviors to move us forward with purpose, meaning, and intention. Unfortunately, we most often do not recognize or take advantage of our thoughts, feelings, and actions because we are caught up in focusing on things outside of our control. Centering on being fed up instead of focusing on what to do about it prevents us from moving forward to resolve the issue(s) and flourish to new heights. The bottom line is we can't be happy, healthy, fulfilled, and ultimately a better version of ourselves until we focus on the option to change what we can control.

A few years ago, I wrote three books using a novel-like self-help format to help people better understand, design, implement, and sustain healthier lifestyle habits. In my books—*Imagine Living Healthier: Mind, Body, and Soul, Destined to Live Healthier: Mind, Body, and Soul*, and *Broken In Plain Sight*—I sought to help people understand the common struggles of living healthier while facing concerns and circumstances related to careers, family, health, finances, and relationships. The encouraging and empowering stories in those books were fashioned to help the reader reevaluate what they prioritized and show ways to reform their unhealthy habits. A change in perspective would leave them refreshed, renewed, rededicated, and ready to balance daily demands, obligations, and pursuits with healthier living, impacting their well-being and work for the better.

This book is an expanded version of my earlier concepts. You will gain insight from familiar road signs on how to answer your "Now what?" You will discover how the right road signs can help you navigate the four steps presented in this book. The steps will help you identify, minimize, and avoid passenger distractions to focus on driving activities and help you reconfigure or create new and expanded roads.

I know these steps have worked in both my personal and professional life. As you read about the four steps, keep four words in your thoughts—move, omit, visualize, and execute (MOVE). You will need to master, omit, visualize, and execute some things. I'm convinced that if you MOVE through each step, you will be happier and more fulfilled in your personal life, your work environment, and your community.

This book provides a lifetime's worth of wisdom and experiences supported by examples from ordinary people who have made some extraordinary roadwork moves. I'm so grateful for the ones God placed in my life at just the right times on my various road journeys. I have been motivated by their acts and inspired to be better as a human resources professional, personal trainer, running coach, author, and community volunteer. They have inspired and impacted my journey to do more and be better. They have used their platforms to help others like me make a difference. I consider these people brilliant as they use their experiences and talents to MOVE. The cards of life weren't always in their favor, and the dice of life didn't always roll on the right number. Whatever challenges life presented them, they never settled nor conceded. They will share nuggets of what they've learned through trials and errors, challenges and uncertainties, and delays and disappointments. Their life experiences will enlighten and support the thoughts in the following pages. Information they share can serve as a guide regarding steps to consider in driving your personal and professional life forward.

Imagine all of us meeting on the road together at rest stops along the way. They are my fav five roadrunners: Ken Johnson, Joyce Johnson, Daniel Henderson, Liletta Harlem, and Anthony Reed. They are on their personal journeys, sharing their roadways. They believe in their potential and that anything is possible. They have been with me during various stages of my journeys, inspiring and empowering me to rise to the next level. I'm so grateful to God for them and the times they chose and afforded me countless times of life-changing opportunities. Throughout the book, you'll understand why I selected these individuals to meet and sit with us at the rest stops.

I hope this book will harness your passion and purpose, inspiring you to take the steps you'll need to MOVE. Like the chirp a smoke alarm makes when it is weak and needs to be replaced, I hope the alerts within this book will sound off in your head as you read and think about the many aspects of your life. I hope you reflect, pause, and look up, down, and all around, assessing aspects of your life that need to be repaired, replaced, or reconfigured.

Each chapter will end with a rest stop exercise. The rest stops include a sign that says, "Be…" Each rest stop "Be…" is created to focus your attention on actions you can take to be a better version of yourself. The corresponding rest stop exercise will provide an opportunity to analyze and write down things you can master, omit, visualize, and execute, and it will guide you on addressing your "right now" and future dreams, initiatives, and pursuits. In the Your Under-Construction Worksheets section, you'll find several worksheets to help you expand your MOVE by planning and acting on what's necessary to flourish beyond your "right now."

Before we start, think about what you are passionate about or something you've always wanted to do or achieve but haven't yet done. Why? Because what you are passionate about, interested in, and/or want to achieve will drive the vision of what you want to accomplish, leaving only the where, when, and how to analyze, plan, and act.

Take a moment and jot down five things you're passionate about, interested in, and/or want to achieve:

_____

_____

_____

_____

_____

Mark this page, and when you finish reading this book, I want you to flip back to it. The actions you take to drive forward and fulfill your passion, interest, and/or achievement will contribute to the legacy you'll leave.

Get ready to *MOVE*!

SELF-ANALYSIS

Chapter 1

Entering Your Under-Construction Consciousness Zone

Who looks outside, dreams;
who looks inside, awakes.

—Carl Jung

Has this ever happened to you?

You approach an intersection and encounter traffic at a standstill. Looking ahead, you see an orange sign stating, "Road closed to thru traffic." Yes, a significant section of the road you've been traveling for years is now under construction. You ask yourself, "Now what?" No need to ask because you see another orange sign that states, "Detour."

The choice has been made for you. You have to take an alternate route, a change that will undoubtedly have a long-term impact on your travel during morning and afternoon peak times to your destinations. You know changes to the road are needed. The problems associated with the road have been clearly identified. The potholes have caused damage to vehicles. You've read about safety concerns with the bridge in this section of the road. The bridge needs to be replaced.

You think, *Man, I've got too much going on at work to have to deal with this detour for the next who knows how long. I don't need the delays getting home after work. The traffic will be a nightmare, and it will increase my gasoline bill! Now is simply not a good time for all of this.* It's a costly inconvenience to take the alternate route each day, but you forget that it's already been costly to your vehicle. You think, *Maybe it'll only last a few weeks.*

You then see signage stating the closure will last through the middle of the following year. Without a doubt, you're frustrated about enduring the impact of the road closure on your life for the next nine months. It'll take so long. You're thinking the completion period for the construction project is not robust enough. Your frustration increases when you realize you'll be cut off from accessing your favorite coffee shop. You're simply fed up with the challenges of the road construction—having to take detours and going way out of your way.

Even if you've never encountered traffic at a standstill or a road under construction, you've experienced something that inspires the same level of mounting stress and domino-effect trials and hardships. These can be things like traumatic childhood memories, family drama, marital problems, friendship betrayal, love difficulties, job concerns, career struggles, financial troubles, health issues, sexual trauma and abuse, and natural disasters. If there were physical customized road signs representing your "right now," they just may read, "I'm tired of being stuck in this long-term parking zone," "No way out of this closed road," "I'm trapped with this passenger," "I'm tired of the same entry and exit ramps," or "I'll never climb out of this drainage hole."

Yes, *I am fed up!*

LIFE UNDER CONSTRUCTION

Think about the roads of your life under construction. Just like a road construction project, there can be many parts, such as planning and designing, project develop-ment, construction, testing, and maintenance. Included in those parts is the completion of background work, which includes an extensive analysis of collected information, project purpose and need, proposed mitigation and enhancements, proposed project delivery, financial impact, and future developments. A lot of work has to be done before the real work—the earthwork—can begin.

The life background, design work, earthwork, paving, and testing you create will start with your self-analysis regarding those road construction sites in your life and what you want your life to ultimately look like. Your next step will be to create the blueprint of the plan you will need to bring your designs to reality. This will give you the ability to shift your thoughts about who you can become in your "right now."

While reading an NBA player's recount of an incident that occurred while he and his four-year-old son were playing basketball, it drove home my thoughts about one's consciousness. The NBA player talked about his son mimicking his (NBA player's) anguished demeanor on the court during a game. While playing basketball, he talked about his son giving him the look and arguing with him like his son saw him (NBA player) do when interacting with the referees.

The NBA player recognized his negative behavior, and he knew he didn't want to make that sort of impression on others. He wanted to be a better example for his son and others watching him. I applaud the NBA player for his consciousness and commitment to being a good example of good behavior for his son and others.

When you create the blueprint for your personal construction, analyzing and identifying the construction sites in your life's road that need to be repaired, replaced, or reconfigured, you won't have a sign telling you which way to go. Something to keep in mind is that you have the control to plan, create, and take as many new and open roads as you need to move your life forward. No road will be absent of detours and delays, but no worries. When you're faced with making a detour, you'll determine how to map new and expanded roads to facilitate continued movement while under construction.

Are you thinking about how long it will last? Too often, we concern ourselves with a completion date. Construction changes and improvements that contribute to evolving us into someone better take time, but just like a road construction project having an associated project plan timeline, you can also have an "under-construction" personal project plan timeline. When you ask, "Now What?" you'll do so as you devise your own robust "under-construction" personal project plan (PPP) so you don't end up frustrated, confused, inconvenienced, angry, or uncertain about the roads you'll travel or the destinations you'll complete.

When I think about my initial personal project plan (PPP), I think about the self-analysis questions I asked myself before getting started. Who am I? Where do I want to go? How is my past impacting my "right now" and my future? At the time, I was in my late twenties, almost thirty years ago. I was unhappy with my job, finances, relationships, and physical appearance. My response to "Who am I?" was, "I am simply existing." My response to "Where do I want to go?" was, "I want to live a life that makes a difference." My response to "How is my past impacting my 'right now' and my future?" was, "It's time to stop harboring things from my past so I can start pursuing things that will lead to having a happy, healthy, and purposeful 'right now' and future."

Answering those questions made pursuing my "Now what?" much easier. At that time, I had the ability to control three things: Analyze, Plan, and Act. I had the ability to identify and analyze the root cause, underlying factors, and effects of my "fed-up" state. I had the ability to create a blueprint to outline my activities and determine needed resources. And I had the ability to act on my plan to MOVE me out of my "fed-up" state.

During one of my first "fed-up" states, I worked for an agency that offered no opportunity for advancement. Every day I reported for work, I dreaded entering the front doors because I knew it would be another day of twiddling my thumbs and looking busy when someone walked past my office door. I thought, *There has to be something greater waiting for me to pursue.*

To MOVE doesn't have to be something elaborate. For me, it was simply researching formats of effective resumes, mastering the contents of my resume, omitting negative thoughts, visualizing career options that interested me, preparing for the interview process, and executing job search efforts. I remember getting the Houston Chronicle newspaper regularly to search the job vacancy announcements. I'm talking about the days when the local newspaper was the primary source for finding a job.

On one particular day, I purchased a Houston Chronicle on my way home after work. Resting in my bed that night, I perused the listing of job vacancies and saw a job listing for a human resource management officer 1, which consisted of recruiter responsibilities for the Texas Department of Criminal Justice. Upon reading the job description, I knew I was an ideal candidate for the position.

As I read about the traveling aspect of the position, I became increasingly excited about traveling throughout Texas and recruiting for one of the state's largest agencies. But there was one problem. The last day to apply for the position was the following day. Now, what do I do? There was only one option. I called my supervisor and informed her that I needed to take the morning off. I left my home first thing the following morning after contacting my supervisor and traveled to Huntsville, Texas (driving distance approximately seventy miles) to complete my hard copy employment application. These were the days of no online applications. I was selected for the position, and my professional human resources life began its evolution.

When I think about the inspirations in my life who urged me to continue analyzing myself and making new life blueprints, I think about Ken Johnson. I met Ken in 1992 when I started working for the Texas Department of Criminal Justice in the human resources (HR) management officer 1 position. He was my immediate supervisor for about two years. Anytime I wasn't traveling and saw Ken in the office, he routinely talked to me about a running group (the Seven Hills Running Club) he co-founded in Huntsville, Texas, in 1985. He also spoke of a book he had written about putting on a race. He rarely missed an opportunity to encourage me to run. When he would invite me to join his running club, I'd politely dismiss the idea. *Not me,* I thought. I wasn't mentally ready to pursue something that sounded physically demanding. In hindsight, I know my "no" had more to do with being stuck on "fed up" in my personal life.

After being under Ken's leadership for two years, I was promoted to another HR position, then eventually promoted again to another HR position that moved me to Dallas, Texas, in 1996. After moving and settling into life in Dallas, Texas, I lost contact with Ken. During that time, my personal life evolved, probably because I was in a new environment removing me from the distractions that kept me emotionally, mentally, and physically stuck. My traveling exposure, while stationed in Huntsville and gleaning new experiences in Dallas, had increased my knowledge on how to master discernment, omit those unhealthy relationships, visualize the difference I wanted to make in society, and execute a variety of action plans.

In 2009, Ultimate HCI Books (a book publishing company) was looking for contributors for its Runner series. The book would feature full-color photography and true stories from beginning runners to Ironman veterans, celebrating what's good (finishing, beating your best time, the wind at your back), bad (morning runs in 32-degree weather, blisters at mile two, no batteries in your iPod), and funny (what's not to laugh about?) about running. I submitted a chapter for consideration, which was selected. I shared my story of how I started running in the book titled, *The Ultimate Runner: Stories and Advice to Keep You Moving.* The title of my story in the book is "Never Give Up: My Journey to Become a Runner."

During the time I was writing my story for the book, I knew I needed to find Ken, who had retired from the Texas Department of Criminal Justice. I needed to share my chapter with him that included how he inspired me to start running. I wanted to share the good news of the fruits from the seed of change he had planted in my head. I simply had to thank him and send him a copy of the book when it was available for sale.

After moving to Dallas and finding my joy of fitness and running, I became a certified personal trainer in November 1997. I then worked part time for Bally's Total Fitness and created my private personal trainer business, BodyShape 2000. I joined a couple of the local marathon training programs. Because of Ken's influence, I entered my first race event, the Dallas Turkey Trot, in November 1998. I later trained for and completed my first marathon, the San Diego Rock 'n' Roll Marathon in May 1999, and my health and fitness journey from that point forward soared.

In January 2002, I kicked off my walk/run program, MAC Fitness (Making-A-Commitment to Fitness), at one of the local parks in Dallas, Texas. Based on the ad I had placed in the local newspaper, the Dallas Weekly, a few people showed and registered for my program. For a couple years, I coordinated and coached the eighteen-week walk/run training program, providing beginner walkers and runners weekly instruction to improve their fitness level and complete—in most cases—their first 5K, 10K, and/or half-marathon race event. For a period of time, I provided fitness tips to the listening audience of 105.7 FM (a local radio station in Dallas, Texas) during the Sunday morning gospel show, hosted by Rev. Adrian Drake and Dr. Sheron Patterson. I participated in health fairs, conducted health and fitness seminars, and received invitations to speak at various conferences about health and fitness.

In 2006, I became a committee member for Kwanzaa, Inc. in Dallas, Texas, founded by Commissioner John Wiley Price. I was appointed to be the race chair and coordinator for an annual event called the KwanzaaFest Beat Obesity 5K Walk/Run in Dallas. My leadership over the 5K event lasted for thirteen years, ending in 2019. From 2008 to 2010, I served as a half-marathon coach for the Crohn's and Colitis Foundation's Team Challenge Program. In 2007 and 2008, respectively, I had self-published *Imagine Living Healthier* and *Destined to Live Healthier*. I also wrote health and fitness articles for a variety of magazines and newsletters.

All my initiatives directly resulted from the seed Ken had planted in my head about becoming a runner. In 2009, I found Ken through an online search, and yes, he was surprised and elated to hear about all I had done because of that seed. In 2010, I would later become the program coordinator and walking coach for Dr. Walton A. Taylor's All About Life Walking Program. It was a walking program that functioned as a community outreach program to provide physical, emotional, and social support to cancer patients.

I have to admit that I would never have imagined that becoming a runner would have such an impact on my life through the years. At the time of writing this book, I have completed eighteen marathons, thirty-plus half-marathons, a plethora of other race events (5Ks, 10Ks, 15Ks, a 30K, and 10-milers), plus coached other individuals to do the same.

In the introduction section, I asked you to think about what you're passionate about. It's okay if you don't know. If you're like me, you'll simply stumble upon your passion. The point I want to make is for you to be conscious about the control you have to analyze yourself, change, and flourish in every aspect of your life.

THE BENEFITS OF SELF-ANALYSIS

When I think about the process of self-analysis, I consider it my opportunity to set the record straight—to be truthful to myself about my reality. Once you face the reality about your who, what, when, where, and how, you can start the process of creating your plans and blueprints to undergo reconstruction and exit your "fed-up" road. You can begin the process of moving your personal and professional life forward to your ideal destination. At the time of my reality check, I was emotionally, mentally, and physically in an unhealthy state. I was stuck. Gripped in toxic lifestyle habits, fractured relationships, and a lack of self-love, my perspective of what really mattered was out of focus. I had to go through the analyzing process to identify the root causes.

GOALS, TARGETS, PURSUITS, AND PRIORITIES

In achieving success with your goals, targets, pursuits, and priorities, your blueprint will require a mastery of the things that can make you better. Consciousness of your daily thoughts, feelings, and behaviors will help you discover what you need to omit, minimizing and eliminating distractions and loss of focus. As you visualize ways to be better in your "right now," you'll discover self-truths and become self-driven. From there, you'll better position yourself to exert the actions and energy necessary to MOVE in your personal and professional life.

Four of my fav five roadrunners are authors. Three of them—Liletta, Tony, and Joyce—talk specifically about events related to their mental and emotional well-being in their recent books.

In her book, *Celebrating A Legacy of Courage and Resolve*, Liletta shares the following: "At age eighteen, I broke up with a guy that I'd been dating for a few years. In fact, we were engaged. I was devastated from that breakup. In my eyes, I was a disappointment to everyone. I don't know if I really wanted to die or if I just didn't know how to live with the pain of disappointment. I just knew that I needed the pain to stop, and I could only think of one way to make that happen. I took many pills and then called a friend. That friend called 911, and I ended up in the hospital. It took a couple of years to recover from that incident. I just didn't feel like I was strong. It was a while before I was glad that my suicide attempt hadn't been successful."

In his book, *From the Road Race to the Rat Race,* Tony shares the following: "I was a mental mess after the suspension, blaming everyone for my failures and becoming deeply depressed. I received the suspension notice between the fall and spring semesters while I was living in the dorm during the Christmas break. I didn't have any place to live after the break was over and didn't have any money or job prospects. I didn't want to return home because my mother and I had a bad relationship. My future goals had been shattered thanks to my overly active social life. I spent the next week taking apart and rebuilding my bicycle while I contemplated my future, feeling suicidal."

In her book, *No Back Doors For Me*, Joyce shares the following: "Working with this company included many firsts for me. I had my first leadership role, my first time being called a killer, my first time seeking counseling due to work-related stress, and my first time taking high blood pressure medication. I think, as African American women, we do a better job than our men when it comes to seeking counseling or taking medication to help level us out. So, to my male readers of any race—take time to take care of yourself as well. The job will be there. Your family needs you here."

Their stories are not unique. They are the comparable stories of many. There's a significant difference though. Amid their situations were moments of self-analysis and blueprinting. They saw themselves as greater than their circumstances.

CONSCIOUSNESS THAT LEADS YOU TO MOVE

A lack of consciousness will stall your progress. Have you ever dreamed of doing something more? Do you constantly talk about your dreams and desires, but something holds you back from taking action to make your dreams a reality? Maybe it's about your past. Maybe someone rejected you or convinced you that you were incapable.

I've listened to people tell me, "I would love to start my own business," "I don't have the discipline to sit down and write a book," "I can't focus long enough to study for that certification," "I wish I had your drive," "I don't have the money to do it," or "I want to be a supervisor in my company." Now think about this. You wake up, brush your teeth, shower, get dressed, brew a cup of coffee or blend the ingredients for your smoothie, and maybe eat something before leaving your home so you can get to work on time. Maybe you do all of that because if you don't, there will be consequences. You know that after being tardy outside what your company's tardy policy allows, you'll get disciplined, and after so many times, you'll be terminated if you're not on time to work. Ensuring you get to work on time qualifies as self-discipline. You are conscious of the consequences. Remember this. You can't move forward if you don't take the first step.

I love a story from Tony's book, *From the Road Race to the Rat Race*, when he talks about his consciousness at an early age in 1968 and the vision it birthed. He shared the following: "As a young history and geography buff, I enjoyed spending hours in the museums and the library. As I walked the hallways, I dreamt of doing something or being famous enough to have an artifact in the museum or my life story in the library. I imagined it would be for science or engineering. Whatever I achieved, it had to be something that could outlive me. It would be my mark on the history of the world."

What a grandiose dream Tony had. It wasn't grandiose for him, though. He knew if he worked hard enough, he'd find a way to make his dream a reality. One of my favorite quotes is by John C. Maxwell, who says, "Dreams don't work unless you do." Tony is a great example of someone who worked toward his dream. Among his many accomplishments, Tony is the first Black person in the world to finish marathons on all seven continents.

In 2012, the National Museum of American History and Culture's curatorial assistant contacted Tony. The Office of Curatorial Affairs had expressed an interest in the artifacts from his international marathons, and he donated several items. Tony wrote in his book, "The museum's construction was completed in 2016. My 1968 dream was capped off when I received a special invitation to attend the museum's pre-opening for the artifact donors on September 17, 2016. I was later interviewed by CNN during the gala." Tony had to master, omit, and execute the actions necessary to make the 1968 dream he had envisioned a reality.

What do you need to do to make your dream a reality? Back when I had become passionate about the world of fitness, I wanted to increase my knowledge about it. As a first step, I enrolled in two different personal trainer certification programs in Dallas, Texas (Baylor Sports Medicine Institute and the Aerobics and Fitness Association of America, AFAA) to obtain my personal trainer certification. Doing so resulted in becoming more knowledgeable, pursuing my passion, and finding my perfect side gig.

When I thought about becoming an author, I looked for a writer's workshop because I didn't know how to write a book. The first event I attended was a Black writer's conference held in Dallas, Texas, in 2006. I learned about writing and publishing from the conference's workshops and seminars. I learned about publishing consultants, editors, publicists, typesetters, distributors, and website designers. I later attended the same conference in 2008 in Tampa, Florida, meeting with authors I'd met at the 2006 conference.

When you have a thought or dream about doing something new or different, one of the first things you should do is research. Look for related books, seminars, conferences, podcasts, special interest groups, and educational institutions to become knowledgeable about the skills and abilities, degree, and/or certification needed to facilitate your dream. Upon having a better understanding of what you need to do, you can include them in your PPP of goals, targets, pursuits, and priorities.

Knowledge and consciousness are your friends. Learn as much as you can about everything, but one word of advice: When you're expanding your knowledge about something, always seek information from a variety of sources. People—whether they're educators, physicians, politicians, experts in a particular field or industry, etc.—have varied opinions when it comes to different subject matters. Those opinions can vary depending on the person's background, education, age, and many other factors. Make sure that whatever decisions you make are informed decisions based on a collection of vetted sources and resources.

YOU'RE CONSCIOUS—NOW IT'S TIME TO MOVE

As a fitness trainer, I remember a conversation with a client who clearly operated in "fed-up" mode. Below is an excerpt of a conversation we had one day:

"Coach, I'm ready. I really mean it this time," Charlotte said, sounding desperate. "I am so tired of feeling like I do. I am so tired of these hot flashes. I am so tired of being fifty-two pounds overweight. I am so overwhelmed with the voices of anxiety, frustration, doubt, and fear in my head. Creating even more anxiety, the other day, a random lady at work asked me if I was pregnant."

"Oh no!" I exclaimed. "Not pregnant!"

"On my birthday next month, I'll be forty-eight. For me, that means another year of not liking the way I look and feel."

"Do you remember the five C's?" I asked.

"Choice. Commitment. Change. Courage. Control?"

"Correct. You did great the first couple months of the year with employing all five. You outlined your plan for becoming physically active, eating healthier, reducing your intake of caffeine, and managing your stress. You walked two to three times a week and had worked your way up to an hour. You were committed to learning how to be creative with cooking healthy meals. You were going to talk to your doctor and research relief options related to hot flashes."

"Yes, I did all of those things. And by doing so, I lost twenty-seven pounds and was feeling better about myself. You helped me to understand how and why I used food as a coping mechanism. Then my efforts came to a screeching halt. Between the stress of changes on my job, leading my church's singles ministry, drama with my mother, and my breakup with Wesley, I didn't have the desire or the energy to focus and continue," Charlotte admitted.

"Sounds like you went back to food as your coping mechanism instead of confronting the distracting issues."

"Yes, I did."

"The components of your life that coincide with the five C's will continue to be a cycle of starts and stops until you address the root causes impacting your ability to maintain consistency. The root causes we tend to stay in denial about will allow negative thoughts, feelings, and actions to slip in and out of your cycle until true transformation takes place."

Charlotte interjected, "Yes, I know. I've been doing talk therapy. My therapist is helping me to dive deeper into my childhood and my relationship with my mother, a conversation that has been difficult for me. Number one, I have to stop living in the past and start living in the present."

Take a moment to think about something or someone you're currently fed up with. Write down the name of that person or thing. Think about why and write it down. That's all for now.

_____

_____

_____

_____

_____

THE IMPACT ON YOUR PROFESSIONAL LIFE

Consciousness is not only something you should address in your personal life. When you're fed up, it may impact your interactions and ability to effectively engage as a team member in an organization or in your own business. Let's imagine you're a business owner or a front-line leader in your organization. The first thing a successful leader does to encourage their team toward individual and team success is get involved. You're in the trenches with the team every day, so it's critical that your team members (individually and collectively) know you're in it together with them to win. You care, you listen, and you are engaged in what's happening in their world (personally and professionally).

If you're stuck in "fed-up" mode, you may not feel like listening, asking, and engaging. You might be going through the motions and waiting for the end of the workday. Talking to your employees routinely about their satisfaction with their roles, the company, and what's meaningful to them will seem more like a chore. And what do we as humans do? We put off doing things that seem like a chore, and they never get done. For the company you work for or the company you own, that means you won't know vital things happening in your employees' world, how they are feeling, and what they need from you to succeed and win. It means you're not building rapport, creating a motivational climate, or showing gratitude. It means you're not having those exploratory coaching conversations that leads to greater trust, better clarification, and a better employee experience. Your "fed-up" state will stifle your ability to check in and ask. Two actions that go a long way toward building a cohesive and successful team. When you authentically listen and show you care—and put your heart and soul in it—people will show up every day engaged and enthused about making an impact and making a difference.

AM I A LEADER?

This question needs to be asked during our conversation about consciousness. Many of you aspire to be a leader in the traditional sense regarding position and title. In my early years working in human resources, I entered the workforce having a certain perspective about a leader. That initial perspective has evolved through the years. While researching for this book, I wanted to gauge the perspective of today's workforce about a leader. I asked a few folks in my circle about their perspective of a leader in their organization. Who did they consider a leader? What was the role of the leader? What was their viewpoint of the leader? What qualified a person to lead? The following summarizes the responses I received.

WHO WAS A LEADER?

Many people I spoke to identified the leader as the president, vice president, c-suite manager (the chief executive officer—CEO, chief financial officer—CFO, chief operating officer—COO, and chief information officer—CIO), politician, department director, superintendent, founder, and so on.

WHAT WAS THE ROLE OF THE LEADER?

Many people spoke of a leader having a vision, building positive relationships, serving others, listening to their team, creating opportunities for their team to shine, ensuring their team has the space and resources to flourish, accepting responsibility when things don't go as planned, and sharing their power, authority, credit, and rewards with others who are within that person's circle of influence.

WHAT WAS THEIR VIEWPOINT OF THE LEADER?

People I spoke with often viewed a leader as someone who should be authentic, flexible, supportive, present, and truthful.

WHAT QUALIFIES A MAN OR WOMAN TO LEAD?

Suggested qualifications of leadership included someone who is promoted, appointed, or elected to president, vice president, c-suite manager, politician, department director, superintendent, and so on.

YOU DON'T NEED A TITLE TO LEAD

Varied perspectives exist regarding who and what makes a leader, but the people I asked didn't consider themselves as leaders. Many of you have the potential to be a leader, but maybe no one has encouraged you to analyze, discover, and pursue your leadership abilities. A leader is somebody who visualizes how to catapult themselves, the team, and business; somebody who listens to and connects with others; somebody who provokes the commitment of others; somebody who is always thinking of the next level; and somebody who can guide people toward a new process or adopt a different approach. When you expand your imagery of a leader, you understand neither a position, title, rank, degree, or certification qualifies anyone to lead other people, nor does age or experience. If you poll people within your circle, there will be commonalities and misconceptions about a leader. Just know, you, too, have leadership potential.

MAKE SURE YOU'RE AN EFFECTIVE LEADER

My early years and first stint of workplace leadership motivated me to analyze who I was. You will do the same because the first person you'll lead is yourself. As an effective leader within my circle of influence and responsibility, I needed to know Bridgette, and doing so involved the following:

- **Self-recognition.** I had to recognize, understand, and accept the truth of my feelings, emotional reactions, drives, viewpoints, perceptions, and beliefs.

- **Self-discipline.** I had to control and manage unfavorable impulses and feelings, defer judgments, and think before acting.

- **Compassion.** I had to understand the emotional makeup, feelings, emotional reactions, drives, viewpoints, perceptions, and beliefs within my team's circle of influence.

- **Motivation.** I had to exert a high level of passion and energy—going beyond the work involving my position, title, and money—to pursue and achieve organizational goals with purpose and confidence.

- **Social skills.** I had to interact and develop relationships that resulted in inclusive and collaborative teams. I had to find commonalities to build rapport and maintain relationships, creating strong bonds to foster constructive conversations and impactful collaboration.

A SUCCESSFUL LEADER IS SELF-DRIVEN

A leader is continuously driven to accomplish above and beyond established expectations. Self-drive is essential when pursuing a next level leadership position in your organization—housekeeping supervisor, team leader, chief accountant, guest services manager, head mechanic, farm manager, school principal, or advertising manager.

Let's explore the state of someone in a leadership position who's not doing so well. We'll start by having the person answer the questions below:

- Is my team stagnant because I am comfortable with the current level of processes, technology, and service levels?

- Do I feel like I'm not worthy of proposing a new initiative or taking the lead on a project?

- Do I allow my perceived personal flaws, problems, and challenges to prevent me from leading my team to greater heights?

- Do I talk myself out of making suggestions to my supervisor about program changes because I believe my abilities, skills, or educational background is less than other team members?

- Do I keep me and my team on the sideline because I am concerned about what others will say or think about me if I speak up?

- Am I fed up with my marriage? Is it affecting my ability to think clearly and discover better ways to lead my team?

To effectively lead a team, you must operate at a high level of self-truths and self-drive—consciousness.

Now is the time to exercise consciousness about your life and self-analyze. Before finding my passion and purpose, I was just going through the motions of life as I went to work, hung out, ran errands, watched television, and wasted money and precious time. Keep in mind that was my perspective of myself because I knew I wanted to do and be more. If you love your life and what it consists of, I'm happy for you. I love this quote by Marthe Troly-Curtin, which says, "Time you enjoy wasting is not wasted time."

For an enhanced perspective on being and doing more, keep reading.

Rest Stop Exercise #1

A BE to Remember: Be Conscious.

Once you become conscious about your who, what, when, where, and how, you can shift and maneuver your lanes of perspectives to exit the "fed-up" road you're on.

M   O   V   E
Master   **Omit**   **Visualize**   **Execute**

What in your "right now" do you need to master to be more conscious about the thoughts, feelings, and actions affecting your who, what, when, and where?

PERSONAL

_____

_____

_____

_____

_____

_____

_____

PROFESSIONAL

_____

_____

_____

_____

_____

_____

_____

What unwanted passengers do you need to omit to facilitate your consciousness?

PERSONAL

_____

_____

_____

_____

_____

_____

_____

PROFESSIONAL

_____

_____

_____

_____

_____

_____

_____

What activities do you visualize to help you improve your consciousness?

PERSONAL

_____

_____

_____

_____

_____

_____

PROFESSIONAL

_____

_____

_____

_____

_____

_____

How will you execute your action plan to be more conscious?

PERSONAL

_____

_____

_____

_____

_____

_____

PROFESSIONAL

_____

_____

_____

_____

_____

_____

NOTES

Chapter 2

Watching Your State of Mind
During Moving Parts

*Seek first the virtues of the mind; and other things
either will come, or will not be wanted.*

—Francis Bacon

As a recruiter for the Texas Department of Criminal Justice, I traveled hundreds of miles throughout Texas to various destinations (big cities and small towns). I tagged every trip as a road trip that would include some sightseeing, so I always packed play clothes. The beauty about a road trip is you can stop along the way and smell the roses. You can take pictures of the scenic views—bluebonnets along the highway. You can visit the town's corner store not just for a restroom break but also to admire the knick-knacks, antiques, crafts, and vintage collectibles. You can stop at places like the town's coffee shop or bakery to buy some of the local favorites.

On my driving trips to small towns in Texas like Fort Stockton, Beeville, Brownsville, Amarillo, El Paso, Palestine, Marshall, and Texarkana, I'd always enjoy the scenic views. Traveling in Texas will provide you with a variety of terrain (desert mountains, limestone hills, rich farmland, grasslands, marshes, deep forests, flat land, rolling hills, and so on). I enjoyed any opportunity to visit the respective city's historic sites. What I didn't enjoy was the hours of solitude while driving, staring ahead at miles of desolate land with no one to talk to and laugh with. This was a time of no expanded cellular telephone service of less traveled roads, so there was no one to call and chat with.

I had periods of physical discomfort because of the stretches of travel in certain areas with no rest stops or gas stations along the way. As a single female traveling alone, stopping on the side of the road was out of the question. Amid trying to stretch my legs while driving and listening to the sounds of country music on the radio stations, I was forced to think about life and the things I wanted to change.

As I reflect on that period of my life, my road travels forced a perfect time for self-analysis and self-reflection. Being separated from the moving parts of my personal life generated opportunities to rediscover suppressed parts of myself, which allowed a first-hand look at different cultures and their way of life while gaining a better perspective on my own life. I think of how I learned to move what I wanted to experience in my life to a place of practice, patience, and peace. Practicing patience would drive me to a place of peace when making decisions about changes I needed to make.

Friends have told me, "Driving takes too long. I fly so I can get to my destination quicker." For those of you who don't mind taking the scenic route, I thought this quote by G.K. Chesterton was appropriate: "One sees great things from the valley; only small things from the peak." I'm always grateful for the opportunities to see and appreciate the small things.

THINK ABOUT YOUR PARTS MOVING YOUR STATE OF MIND

Sometimes, you have to do some drainage work and clear the moving parts affecting your ability to think clearly, evolve, and grow. How would you rate your state of mind? What do you need to clear? Do you need to reconcile the volt of memories in your mind that house the good, bad, and the ugly? What about emotional trauma where the wounds are still raw? In some cases, it's a rawness that still exists decades later, where the choice to forget and/or forgive is unsettled. Are you still holding on to someone or something comparable to the following?

- A parent who has always dismissed, discredited, or denied you.
- The classmate who bullied you.
- The backlash you received because of the neighborhood where you were raised.
- The lingering conflict from your marriage that ended years ago.
- A spouse who cheated on you.
- The boss who recommended your termination from a job.
- A romantic partner who stole money from you.
- A partner who left you in financial ruin.
- A boss who made your life in the workplace a living hell.

There comes a time when we all must do some soul searching and self-analysis, which goes a long way in clearing the aforementioned moving parts. One of my favorite quotes is a quote I heard on a TV show, "Sometimes we have to visit with our past before we can pack it up and store it away." We must heal from the ghosts of our past that haunt us so we can move forward in peace and purpose. If we don't, consequences for repeated behaviors will be the catalyst of our past and the inability to resolve it. The ultimate consequence is that any ambitions we may have to discover and pursue our rightful place in society are blocked by unsettled emotional trauma. Having the right state of mind will positively impact your personal well-being—emotional, mental, physical, and social.

When I think about emotional, mental, physical, and social well-being as an older and wiser female, I'm more focused than ever on living my "right now" with peace, joy, and contentment mixed with fun and adventure. Above all, I want to help others acknowledge their "right now," understand their purpose, and pursue being better in all aspects of their lives. I want that for you too. Find the peace, joy, and contentment amid your life's demands, obligations, stresses, uncertainties, unfulfillments, criticisms, and disappointments. Reconcile the volt of memories in your mind that house the good, bad, and the ugly, then help those in your circle of influence to do the same.

In preparation for 2021, my best running friend, Tracy, gave me a journal called the "Contentment Journal." It instructs its reader to commit ninety days to a journey that will not only lead toward contentment but ultimately help with the discovery of joy in one's life. After receiving the journal, I called Tracy, and we talked about the introductory language in it.

The first sentence read, "What's the first thing you do in the mornings?" Tracy and I chuckled about the author's admittance of scrolling through her social media. I shared proudly with Tracy that since July 1, 2020, the first thing I did in the mornings was read a bible chapter. Doing so had added value to my mental state, but I knew I missed something due to my inability to successfully focus on my ambitions, and you should never run out of having ambitions. Tracy and I discussed the pitfalls of starting the morning scrolling social media. I could relate because prior to July 1, 2020, it was how I started my morning—scrolling my timeline to see what everyone shared from the night before. In November 2020, a light bulb went off in my head and I had a consciousness moment. I concluded that scrolling social media stifled my present-day "Now what?"

When I asked Liletta about the moving parts in her life she had omitted that she considered a hinderance to her growth and state of mind, she shared the following: "I've omitted time wasters. And this is hard because some time wasters are things that help. For example, being on social media is necessary for my work; however, if not careful, it becomes too much and takes up a lot of time. So, by putting time limits on how often I go on and utilizing a team to help with making posts, it allows me to keep it under control."

As I wrote this book, I wanted to equip my readers with the understanding that they must first have internal joy before successfully positioning themselves to plan for their "Now what?" Mastering your state of mind and clearing those moving parts will make you well-equipped at research, analyses, critical/strategic thinking, and decision-making in both your personal and professional life. Road signs I'll typically see when driving through a construction zone include wording like, "Stay Alert. Drive Now. Talk and Text Later." That's a sign we need in our personal lives to help us minimize distractions and stay focused on moving and reaching our destinations safely.

Think about what moving parts hinder your personal growth and write it here. For now, I simply want you to be conscious about that someone or something.

_____

_____

_____

_____

_____

THE IMPACT ON YOUR PROFESSIONAL LIFE

You don't have to be an executive leader within a company to lead. A leader can occur at every level of an organization, whether you're a department head in a government agency, a team leader at a fast-food restaurant, the sales manager for a marketing company, the person who influences others, or the person who works with others to achieve a goal. Oftentimes, employees who are singular top performers, creators, and innovators are selected or appointed to fill titled leadership roles; however, they may not be prepared to perform under the conditions a titled leader may face when leading a team of people. You might have the demonstrated competencies, but are you ready for the conditions? Those conditions will likely include workplace adversities, challenges, roadblocks, and setbacks.

When I entered the workforce right out of college, I wanted to be a leader. Why not? I had gotten a business management degree, which meant I was equipped to lead people and business operations. When my first opportunity with the Texas Department of Criminal Justice arrived, one of the first books I read was *The 7 Habits of Highly Effective People* by Stephen R. Covey. That book became a resource book for me, and I have always referred back to it for a refresher on the author's insights on change and creating opportunities. Another book I used as a resource was *The Art of Managing People* by Dr. Phillip Hunsaker and Dr. Anthony Alessandra.

In 1995, my leadership opportunity arrived. And you know what? I wasn't ready. Sure, I was a great recruiter. Sure, I had a solid reputation for creating, developing, and producing results. Sure, I contributed to the development and transformation of specialty recruitment programs and services. Sure, I had read some great books. But to lead a team of people? I wasn't ready.

I went from being a specialized employment recruiter, having never led a team, to being an assistant regional human resources administrator. The agency did spend several weeks training other new regional administrators and me on technical and conceptional skills related to setting up and operating a regional human resources office in a new city. We trained on the activities related to the delivery of varied human resources programs and services, along with interviewing, selecting, hiring, and training staff.

Ultimately, I managed twenty-seven human resources team members in the regional and related field offices. During the selection process for staffing the regional office, I was excited about the individuals we hired. I saw myself doing leadership activities: motivating them, keeping them informed, supporting them, collaborating with them, and providing valuable feedback. I had read the right books and received the necessary training, and I was ready for my inaugural leadership journey—at least, I thought so. The new regional human resources office was opened in early 1996.

In less than ten months of opening the regional human resources, I received notification of an EEO (equal employment opportunity) complaint against me from an employee I thought I had a good relationship with. As you would expect, my state of mind would have been described as frustrated and off-kilter after being accused of retaliation and discrimination based on religion. Again, this was my first role as a titled leader.

To share a little something about the complainant, after numerous complaints from field employees, I discovered errors the complainant employee had been making and hiding related to our insurance program. The EEO complaint came after the complainant employee had been counseled, then given a letter of corrections due to his poor job performance. I knew I hadn't violated any retaliation or discrimination laws, but the investigation process was stressful.

To grow, you must know and accept what you don't know. I knew I needed to expand my knowledge of the Equal Employment Opportunity Commission (EEOC) and its responsibility for enforcing federal laws that make it illegal to discriminate against a job applicant or an employee because of the person's race, color, religion, sex (including pregnancy, transgender status, and sexual orientation), national origin, age (forty or older), and disability or genetic information. I knew I had to master a new set of skills—technical skills related to Title VII of the Civil Rights Act of 1964. I researched and gathered resources (to include the federal agency responsible for administering and enforcing civil rights laws—EEOC) to increase my knowledge and facilitate my technical knowledge about such a critical area.

I wanted to make sure I was the best I could be in my new leadership role. I created and moved forward with a plan to dissect my position, its functions, responsibilities, and requirements. I visualized what the optimal operation of the department looked like. I executed my action plan to establish authority without trying to over-control or micromanage. I worked to reinforce my team's confidence in me as their supervisor. I established goals and expectations for myself and the team members. I utilized the progressive disciplinary process when those times arose, and it was necessary to help my employees correct behavior concerns and resolve performance issues in the beginning stages. I worked to ensure my employees felt respected, understood, and valued. My state of mind transitioned from frustrated to focused.

The investigation was completed, and I received my investigative outcome letter stating: "We reviewed all of the information and documents gathered in the investigation and have concluded that the complaint is unsubstantiated." The employee was later terminated from the agency.

Several years later, I would end up writing the progressive corrective action and related disciplinary policies and procedures for my agency, and I facilitated the development of related training programs. Twenty-plus years later, I would become a specialized HR investigator for the third-largest school district in Texas. Yes, I became the person who investigated allegations of discrimination, harassment, and retaliation.

During my years in the workforce, I understood that having the right state of mind in the workplace is important because, at some point, you'll face difficult situations as both an employee and a leader. You don't want to make decisions when you're feeling stressed and anxious. You must practice a positively focused thought process while encountering a variety of moving parts. You want your focus to be on having a state of mind where you possess clarity, calmness, peace, and patience in all situations. While it's an easy statement to make when you don't consider the things in your life outside of the workplace, you may experience external factors like the following:

- Your financial report is due today, but you're stressed about having to leave your sick baby with a family member.
- You're scheduled to meet with a sought-after financial investor, but you're distraught because last evening, your dog was struck and killed by a truck.

- You're the top sales associate currently training a new group of sales associates for your company, but you're having difficulty accepting the fact you've been served divorce papers.

- You've been selected as the lead consultant over a construction project that will require you to be multi-focused, but you're distraught about your young child's recent cancer diagnosis.

Although the situations are beyond your control, you are in control of maintaining clarity, calmness, and peace as you carry out your work obligations. Maintaining a positive state of mind in your professional life ensures employee engagement, the customer's experience, employee productivity, creativity, and organizational goals will not be impacted.

AN EXPANDED STATE OF MIND PERSPECTIVE

When I thought about the platforms of my fav five roadrunners, I wondered about their perspective on having the right state of mind. They are people I told you about who would be at the rest stop with us. Sidenote: Whether it's a mentor, some positive person who crosses your path, or a role model who contributes to helping you move your life forward, you want those people in your life. Their actions, activities, and achievements will inspire and serve as reminders of how you can start moving forward on your journey amid the moving parts.

I love my fav five roadrunners because of their lifelong commitment to making a difference and their lifelong dedication to learning creative ways to be better. They challenge me to consider new perspectives that will give me a more positive and fruitful state of mind. They are people I trust. You, too, want to align yourself with people who contribute to your improvement and growth. I'll share more about having the right people in your inner circle in Chapter 6.

Check out the perspectives Joyce, Daniel, Liletta, and Tony have shared about having the right state of mind:

- **Joyce:** Right state of mind for me is also a matter of the heart. I know people who create amazingly profitable businesses; however, they are not attached. It's a matter of revenue. I know I can't dedicate my full energy to a space that doesn't also connect to my heart. So I must be clear on both mind and heart to facilitate change.

- **Daniel:** Having the right state of mind has helped me achieve many of my goals. I know God has played a big role in my life. Anytime I am going through something, I see Him working with me to provide me with the right state of mind to try and make the right decision in my personal and professional growth. God has placed quality people in my life that I can talk to about my decision-making process.

- **Liletta:** The first word that comes to mind is calm, followed by peace. For me, this is when I know that I'm in the right space to make clear decisions and effective personal growth. When I feel anxious and uneasy, then I need to reset before I can truly have the space of clarity that I need.

- **Tony:** From years of being a distance runner, I've learned to find peace in the middle of chaos. When you're in a race, your opponents are trying to chase you down. You're completely tired, and you must learn to relax and focus on your objective. If you look defeated, your opponent may sense it and go for the kill. Thus, you must be able to (mentally) quickly go to a peaceful place and focus on relaxing your body and mind while looking for creative solutions while under pressure.

Think about something that hinders your professional growth. Write it here. For now, I simply want you to be conscious about that someone or something.

_____

_____

_____

_____

_____

Poor drainage causes distress, which can lead to your inability to mitigate the impact of your unwanted passengers, causing forward movement problems and failures while under construction. To prevent or minimize failures and ensure completion of your goals, targets, pursuits, and priorities, it is imperative to conduct adequate drainage. Your PPP will help you do the drainage work necessary, clearing the moving parts affecting your ability to think clearly, evolve, and grow.

Rest Stop Exercise #2

A BE to Remember: Be Focused.

Have you ever stopped to watch the clouds in the sky? If so, you noticed how they constantly move, modify, and take different forms. Our thoughts are no different, constantly moving, modifying, and taking different forms. The ability to focus on one thing at a time is necessary for succeeding at work and in life. To do something well, you must be able to concentrate on it. You must practice focusing on being refocused. Doing so will contribute to becoming and sustaining focus.

What in your "right now" do you need to master to be
more focused on having the right state of mind?

PERSONAL

_____

_____

_____

_____

_____

_____

_____

PROFESSIONAL

_____

_____

_____

_____

_____

_____

_____

What unwanted passengers are impeding your focus?

PERSONAL

_____

_____

_____

_____

_____

_____

PROFESSIONAL

_____

_____

_____

_____

_____

_____

What action activities do you visualize to help you focus?

PERSONAL

_____

_____

_____

_____

_____

_____

PROFESSIONAL

_____

_____

_____

_____

_____

_____

How will you execute your action plan to be more focused?

PERSONAL

_____

_____

_____

_____

_____

_____

PROFESSIONAL

_____

_____

_____

_____

_____

_____

NOTES

Chapter 3

Capturing Your Personal Core Values While Under Surveillance

Try not to become a person of success, but rather try to become a person of value.

—Albert Einstein

I remember when I was fifteen and studying the *Texas Driver Handbook*, preparing myself for the written test to obtain my driver's license. I read about traffic laws, road signs, examples of common driving situations, and general safety tips. Two core values I learned were accountability and respect—personal accountability for road safety and decisions I'd make, and respect while sharing the road with others.

If you're like me, you've probably had some lapses through the years when it comes to exercising good judgment while driving on the roads. These might include things like driving in excess of the posted speed limit, honking your horn at people, or texting while driving. There have been times when I've had to revert back to practicing and maintaining what matters most—good old-fashioned values.

WHAT YOU STAND FOR MATTERS

What do you stand for? Because what you stand for is your responsibility. Your reality for what you stand for will be shaped by your personal core values, which will ultimately represent your character. People whose personal core values have not been shaped—or if they lose their way along the way—can end up making bad decisions. When I think about actions I've observed or heard about, I think about the following:

- The person who destroys another person's personal property to get revenge.
- The person who bullies or treats someone differently because of their race, ethnicity, age, religion, or disability.

- The person who places an object in their plate of food at a restaurant to avoid paying for the meal.
- The person who hides their car to prevent it from being repossessed.
- The person who inflates their income to acquire a purchase they can't afford.
- The person who receives a package at their home, it was delivered to the wrong address, and the person keeps it.
- The person who knowingly hits a person walking on a dark and isolated street and keeps going.

GOOD OLD-FASHIONED VALUES SHOULD NEVER RUN OUT OF STYLE

To be a leading light with your family and friends, in your work environments, and in your inner circle of influence, you must have a clear and present mindset about your personal core values, which comprises your foundational beliefs. They influence your behaviors and guide you to make good, steady decisions. Even if you have some lapse in exercising good judgment, a solid understanding of what constitutes your good personal core values will cause you to pivot, get back on track, and do the right things. We simply have to repave our core values.

Children, teenagers, and adults can observe behaviors and perspectives from a variety of sources that have the propensity to shape their personal core values. These sources include parents, television, educational institutions, religious organizations, social media, books, friends, classmates, and family members. As a child growing up in the '70s, I don't remember a targeted discussion about values in my household. What I do remember is my parents, in their own way, teaching me values like being kind, courteous, respectful, thoughtful, responsible, and grateful. They were my parents' to-dos, and as I reflect on the values they talked about, they included being kind, courteous, respectful, and thoughtful toward others. These translated into actions like:

- greeting people with a smile;
- saying good morning/afternoon/evening;
- saying excuse me to politely get someone's attention or express regret;
- speaking up during an interaction with someone;
- responding to elders with "yes, ma'am/sir" or "no, ma'am/sir";
- saying "please" when requesting something;
- saying "thank you" verbally and in writing to show appreciation;
- opening/holding the door for someone;
- offering a seat to a pregnant or an elderly person; and

- valuing the property of others.

Being responsible translated into actions like:

- doing what I'll say I'll do, and if I can't, letting the person know I can't;
- wearing clean clothing, like under garments;
- using deodorant every day;
- brushing my teeth and checking my breath;
- paying church tithes/offerings;
- keeping my room/house clean;
- knowing my physical address and the household telephone number;
- studying to make good grades in school;
- practicing the piano and clarinet to become better;
- counting my money before I leave the store;
- adhering to motor vehicle driving rules;
- reporting to work on time;
- listening to my superiors;
- doing a good job at work;
- accepting responsibilities for mistakes;
- making wise spending decisions;
- living within the salary I was making;
- balancing my checkbook;
- paying bills by the due date;
- establishing and maintaining good credit;
- saving money for a rainy day;
- paying attention to the road while driving;
- steering away from driving under the influence of alcohol or drugs;
- avoiding following the crowd;
- paying a traffic ticket or any criminal violation by the due date;
- buying gas for the car;
- getting routine car maintenance checks;
- understanding the basics for how to fix a flat tire;
- maintaining adequate car insurance coverages;

- making sure a spill I made was cleaned up properly;
- filling the ice tray when it's empty;
- throwing my gum away in a trash can and not on the ground;
- covering my mouth/nose when I coughed/sneezed; and
- never taking anything without authorization that doesn't belong to me.

Being grateful translated into actions like:

- acknowledging and showing both verbal and physical appreciation, such as a hand-written thank-you card or note, or a token (gift card, fruit basket, flowers, or book) for something said or done. I'll share more about gratitude in Chapter 7.

I'm sure you have your list of dos and don'ts instilled in you. Back then, I believe my parents' value system was to ensure I was kind, courteous, and self-reliant; a good decision maker; a good manager of money to handle financial obligations; and someone who did not do anything that would lead me (or them on my behalf) to have to navigate the criminal justice system.

Their foundation of values served me well on so many different levels, academically and artistically, especially when I entered the workforce at sixteen. My first job as a teenager was with Joske's Department Store at Northline Mall in Houston, Texas. I still vividly remember my dad having the talk with me. Of course, the talk included reporting to work on time, listening to and following the instructions of my supervisor, and doing a good job. But because he knew I'd have access to money and merchandise, he also talked to me about stealing and what the consequences of a bad decision involving theft would mean. More importantly, he talked to me about friends wanting me to give them free stuff, and I didn't think much about his talk involving that. At the age of sixteen, my friends consisted of my cousins, the church kids, a couple of the neighborhood kids, and my high school classmates. None who would ever ask me to give them free stuff from my job.

I simply responded, "Yes, sir. Okay." All I knew was that I could earn my own money, buy the name-brand polo shirts, and get a store discount on my purchases. You see, my parents didn't believe in spending money on name-brand clothing items. So, if I wanted such, I had to figure out how to get them.

Well, one day, the unimaginable happened. A group of girls I attended elementary school with saw me working in the women's department at Joske's. They were not friends by any means. One of the girls was someone who bullied me in elementary school. She approached me and asked me to give them some clothing items, continuing her request by saying, "Nobody will know." Without hesitation or procrastination, and holding fast to my values, I adamantly said "*No.*" Whatever else I said to the girls and the tone I said it with ensured I never had that request or encounter ever again because they understood my values and where I stood.

FAMILY VALUES MATTER

In the present day, a discussion about personal core values is a topic too important for a parent or someone with parental responsibility not to have directly with their child. Your values become family values. As a kid growing up in the '70s and '80s, we had wholesome old-school television shows that were both entertaining and educational with life lessons filled with common-sense advice, reconciliation, integrity, and respect. My favorites included *The Andy Griffith Show*, *Leave It To Beaver*, *Hazel*, *Father Knows Best*, *The Brady Brunch*, and *My Three Sons*. I love this quote by H. Jackson Brown, Jr., who says, "Live so that when your children think of fairness, caring, and integrity, they think of you."

In her book, *Celebrating A Legacy of Courage And Resolve,* Liletta shared a memory about a time she was untruthful as a child. She recounted a conversation her mother had with her about lying, "She gave me a nice, long story about lying. She hated lying, and she explained how lying and trust were connected. My mom is a talker, so this was no short conversation. I still remember the illustration she gave me at the time. She told me that if someone ever said something bad about me, and she asked me if it was true, if I was known as a liar, she'd never be able to prove that I was innocent. She wouldn't know if I was lying! Man, did I feel terrible! I had lied, and my mom couldn't even trust me! Mommy let that illustration sink in."

During a conversation with a friend of mine, he shared his disappointment about a family member. He talked about the death of his sister and wanted to purchase a headstone for her grave. He asked his sister's son if he wanted to contribute to the purchase of the headstone. His nephew indicated he would contribute. My friend moved forward with purchasing a headstone for his sister's grave. His disappointment was that his nephew started avoiding his telephone calls when the time came to contribute.

My friend and I talked about values and what they mean historically. We're both from the generation of "your word is your bond," which simply means a person will always do what he or she has promised to do. My friend and I talked about a value that is high on our list, which is integrity—knowing and doing what is right. If someone says they are going to do something, it is a commitment or promise they will keep, with no written agreement or contract filled with terms and conditions needed. When a person is committed to sticking to their values, doing so allows that person to not suffer the bad feelings, guilt, and burden that comes along with dismissing or avoiding a commitment.

None of us are perfect. Life can be a series of trial and error, but when we make commitments and promises, a good habit to practice is making sure we honor our commitments and promises. If we're unable to do that, then simply say it. So, did my friend's nephew agree to contribute to the headstone knowing he had no intention of contributing? Did his nephew simply forget about his word to contribute? If so, he probably wouldn't have avoided my friend's telephone calls. Did something change financially with my friend's nephew that left him too embarrassed to let my friend know he was unable to contribute? In the words of my friend, "I hate my nephew felt he had to ghost me. If he was unable to contribute, all he had to do was be honest and let me know."

I love the perspectives Joyce, Daniel, Liletta, and Tony have shared about personal core values:

- **Joyce:** Trust! Because trust drives integrity, respect, accountability, and all above. People trust you if you lead with the above. That's how you get to trust.

- **Daniel:** My core values are treating people with respect and integrity. Also, understanding I have to be accountable for failures and success in business and life. I believe that being honest about your opinions related to business and life can only build better relationships. If the relationships end, you can lean on your integrity to understand you treated the relationships with a great deal of respect.

- **Liletta:** Honesty and gratitude. I've gotten to a point in my life where being honest to myself and to others while staying in a space of true gratitude is the only way I can function or manage my depression and anxiety. By truth, I don't mean simply stating something that happened, for example, but truth that is steeped in gratitude. Like a truth statement might be that we grew up poor, but that isn't necessarily connected to gratitude. How I would rephrase that is to say I grew up learning survival skills and how to appreciate even the smallest of things because we didn't always have the resources and funds to get what we wanted, but we always had what we needed.

- **Tony:** Being realistic. If I lie to myself about a problem situation, then I'll implement the wrong solution. I have to be honest and realistic with myself at all times.

DEMONSTRATED ACTIONS OF A "FED-UP" STATE

These are some actions of people I've heard about or witnessed, such as:

- the customer who curses at a sales associate in front of other customers because she believes a garment is not priced correctly;

- a citizen who makes obscene comments to a government clerk because they were instructed to complete the correct form;

- a heated argument between two customers because one got the last container of Clorox;

- a driver who throws their middle finger up in the air toward another driver because the driver did not let their car pass;

- the parent who yells at school board members about a rule change in front of their kid;

- the fan of an NBA team who, during a playoff game, spits on a player from the opposing NBA team;

- a man shaking his fist at the service advisor inside the auto shop because he believes someone stole money out of his center console; and

- the girlfriend pounding and kicking on her boyfriend's front door, trying to break it in.

I think, *That person is allowing the roots (someone and/or something) of their "fed-up" state to exist and persist through bad behaviors.* These same individuals are employees, team members, managers, supervisors, and business owners. They are possibly parents who are exhibiting bad behaviors in front of their child(ren) that could end up being generational. If you or someone you know are having a difficult time managing the stresses in your life, which continues to allow the roots of the "fed-up" state to grow, seek help with people like the pastor at your church, the employee assistance program through your job, the National Alliance on Mental Illness, the National Institute of Mental Health, or Mental Health America.

CHAOS AND YOUR PERSONAL CORE VALUES

An unstable and misguided foundation of personal core values can lead to getting caught up in chaos—a three-ring circus of crazy when dealing with your family, friends, and people in your work environment. During chaos, we often make impulsive and desperate decisions. The impulsive and desperate decisions allow us to settle into unhealthy and unfruitful relationships, buried in financial debt, or listening to and trying to please people who don't have our best interest at heart.

The longer you allow chaos to linger in your life, the deeper the emotional, mental, physical, and social scars will last and settle. Have you ever had a scar that just wouldn't go away? You used cocoa butter or some bleaching cream, and neither would work. It could be because you kept picking at the scar, making it deeper. Nothing changed because you kept picking at it. Well, that's how the chaos in our lives work. If we keep picking at and feeding chaos, letting it linger around, it will not leave, and it could result in you living a continued life of convenience, comfort, complacency, commotion, confusion, and conflict. No worries, you can choose your clearing process.

PRACTICE GOOD CORE VALUES

Your values are comprehensive beliefs that can be reapplied many times in your life within various situations to guide your actions. Checking your personal core values and mastering those you want to reflect your foundational beliefs is paramount. Practicing good personal core values can help you clear out the chaos.

DEFINE YOUR PERSONAL CORE VALUES

Let's take a look at some examples of personal core values that can positively support the actions of your character.

- HUMOR – being amused by something seen, heard, or thought about
- GRATITUDE – being appreciative for what you receive, whether tangible or intangible
- INTEGRITY – knowing and doing what is right
- RESPECT – showing consideration and regard for others
- CIVILITY – being polite and courteous when you speak and act
- COMPASSION – being kind and considerate and showing concern for the well-being of others
- ACCOUNTABILITY – safeguarding all entrusted opportunities and contributions
- DEPENDABILITY – doing what you say you will do
- RELIABILITY – doing what others expect of you
- LOYALTY – standing by one's side in good and bad times
- COMMITMENT – being steadfast to a promise or agreement
- OPEN-MINDEDNESS – listening to the ideals of others without bias or judgment
- CONSISTENCY – demonstrating courageously all of the above in all situations

What personal core values stood out to you? Take a moment and choose your top five, then describe why they are important to you.

_____

_____

_____

_____

_____

INTEGRITY MATTERS

Did integrity make your list? Integrity is always a big one for me. When you're on the road of life, integrity is your personal compass and will influence the kind of person you become over time. A good practice is to frequently ask yourself why you made your decisions. It's important to always be honest with yourself. It lets you get to know and realize your motives.

As you think about integrity, think about the following:

Have you ever lied about something in the workplace? Write about a time that has happened. Be honest and share with yourself how you would do things differently in the future.

_____

_____

_____

_____

_____

Have you ever stood alongside your boss and listened to him or her lie about something? Maybe your boss altered the numbers—the data—related to a report and presented a false or enhanced narrative. Write about a time. Be honest and share your reaction or action. Share with yourself how you would do things differently in the future.

_____

_____

_____

_____

_____

A belief system including integrity will influence you to do the right thing, such as telling the truth even when the truth does not present something in the best light. I love this quote by Philip Johnson: "Admitting one's own faults is the first step to changing them, and it is a demonstration of true bravery and integrity."

Let's think about a hypothetical situation. Even though I know you'll never find yourself in this situation, humor me. Let's say you or a coworker manipulated and lied about critical data on a business report you prepared. A team member discovered the manipulated data. What did you do? Were you in harmony with the values prompting you to take responsibility for your actions? Write about a time. Be honest.

_____

_____

_____

_____

_____

HONEST CONVERSATIONS

Oftentimes, the lack of open and honest communication in our personal lives can lead to a lack of open and honest communication in professional lives. I'm sure you've heard someone make this statement about a leader in the organization: "He/she says one thing one day, then says something totally different the next day." Even in the midst of your "fed-up" state, you want to make sure you're acting in a capacity that promotes honest conversations and good, steady decisions. You never want to do something where your integrity and judgment are challenged.

THE IMPACT ON YOUR PROFESSIONAL LIFE

To grow and mature as a leader, I needed to define and outline my core values. Your values will shape your behaviors and influence how you lead. The value list I shared earlier in this chapter—integrity, respect, accountability, reliability, and open-mindedness—is mine.

IMPORTANT BEs IN THE WORKPLACE

When I think about some of the human resources cases I've investigated, I think about things like:

- the police officer fabricating evidence,
- the accountant fixing numbers,
- the employee stealing money from the office's petty cash box,
- the teacher changing a student's grades,
- the truck driver delivering a package containing drugs,
- the government clerk stashing cash payments, and
- the government official taking gifts from a company representative who wants a government contract.

My core values influence my behaviors or the BEs I want to *be* as a leader of myself and to others within my circle of influence and responsibility. They are not in any particular order. I use BE to keep me locked in and focused on being better today, tomorrow, and every day.

- BE present.
- BE focused.
- BE strategic.
- BE committed.
- BE collaborative.
- BE solutions-oriented.
- BE reliable.
- BE respectful.
- BE healthy.
- BE grateful.

Yes, I have a lot of BEs. My BEs have contributed to bettering myself as a person and a leader.

Being present is one of my favorite BEs. If you're not present, your other BEs will be impacted. Oftentimes, our present is filled more with the past than with the here and now, so if you're not present, then where are you? Are you thinking about something that happened in your past? Are you thinking about something that is going to happen in your future? We typically think about a person not being present when they appear to be reading an email during a meeting, texting someone during a speaker's presentation, or watching television while someone is talking. All of this has an impact on those nearby during your non-present state. They feel ignored, unheard, and frustrated.

Think about a specific time you were not present and describe the situation. What was the impact of not being present? What did you learn?

_____

_____

_____

_____

_____

Another important BE of mine is to be focused. One of my favorite things to do is attend a bodyworks class at my local gym. I don't have to think about not being present. I have no other choice. Because for fifty-five minutes, all I have to do is focus my attention on Kim, my instructor. My mind doesn't have an opportunity to wander. I have to be present to move with Kim and get the results I want from the class.

Through my fitness class, I learned how to be better at being focused as a leader. For starters, I practice conscious presence. If my mind starts to wander as I'm engaging with others, I bring attention back into focus. By making sure I'm focused on the now, it ensures I'm present when talking to someone like a client, colleague, or employee. As a leader, my primary goal is to be focused, more intentional, and purposefully in the moment as I'm collaborating with, guiding, or supporting others. I want to make sure I'm listening to understand and then act appropriately. Doing so leads to enhanced relationships with colleagues, peers, employees, managers, supervisors, customers, and clients.

Think about a specific time when you had to focus. Describe the situation. What was the impact of being focused? What did you learn?

_____

_____

_____

_____

_____

The good news is that you can choose the personal core values you want to represent your character and guide your behaviors and decisions. Think of your personal core values as your brand. For many employees, the idea of developing and building a personal brand is unknown. When a conversation about "brand" is initiated in the workplace, it is typically related to the company's brand. You, the employee of a company, must also see yourself as a "brand." Everything you do in the workplace is evaluated by your supervisors, your peers, and your subordinates based on the way you communicate with others, what you wear, how you walk, what you say about your supervisor and the organization, and your ability to do your job. Just like a company, you want to be clear about who you are, what you do, and what you want to be known for. You are a person who has been gifted with diverse talents. The BEs shared throughout this book can help you create, develop, and implement a brand that will impress the decision-makers in the organization. A great goal to have is to progress your career and ensure your diverse talents are recognized both within and beyond the walls of your company. Seize every opportunity to showcase your diverse talents. You're not bragging, you're simply self-promoting.

MAKE SURE YOUR PERSONAL VALUES ALIGN WITH YOUR COMPANY'S VALUES.

When we enter the workplace, we'll see the company's values posted somewhere that will include statements like the following:

- Act with integrity.
- Do the right thing.
- Make something better today.
- Deliver outstanding results.
- Continuously improve.
- Operate with transparency.

- Make a difference every day.
- Find a better way.
- Build Relationships/Deliver Results.
- Customer first.
- Help each other thrive.
- Deliver on our commitments.
- Exceed the expectations of our customers and your colleagues.
- Have fun.

It's important to work for a company whose values align with your personal core values. Those shared values will contribute to you being a happy and satisfied employee. You are probably saying to yourself, "Company values aren't important to me. I want a fulfilling job with a good salary." I'd agree with fulfilling and the right salary.

When I'm consulting with an individual about their career progression, one thing I like to consider is the job they applied for. During the time I actively searched for a new job, I'd research the company that interested me. Regarding one of the companies, I noticed that every few months, the same job would resurface on the company's job vacancy list. Based on my research and the level of the position, I knew the vacancy wasn't because of the company's growth. It was evident that the position underwent a constant turnover. That was a red flag to me, as something in the organization may have caused the turnover. When you're applying for a new job, it's important to base your decision on whether the job will be challenging and exciting. It's also important to look at the compensation package, but it's also important to consider the company's core values.

I've seen many great company value statements, but I know many companies don't create platforms where the leadership spends time with employees to explain the intent behind the company's stated values. There may also be a lack of expounding upon their expectations. They state the values but don't live the values. If companies don't take the time to discuss values and expectations—values and expectations that may not have been instilled in the employee as a child or adult—the examples of unfavorable actions below will become the norm rather than the exception.

- A video of a law enforcement officer taking disturbing aggressive actions toward another human.
- A news report about a passenger knocking out the front teeth of a flight attendant because the passenger did not want to adhere to the requirement of wearing a mask.

In both cases, personal core values may have never been introduced or taught to them.

If they were introduced, the actions of the officer and passenger would represent a lapse in good judgment. As adults, we must determine what is of most value to us. We can't allow any bubbling of emotions under the surface because when that boiling point is reached, our triggered reactions can have dire consequences in our professional lives. On the other hand, when there is harmony and alignment between personal and company values, success is more easily found in every aspect of our lives.

Having a solid foundation of core values will contribute to making you a better employee, leader, or business owner. I started my list with humor because I believe that in spite of what's going on in your life, it's important to find humor along with a smile and laughter.

Rest Stop Exercise #3

A BE to Remember: Be Value-Focused.

The lack of good personal core values will affect every aspect of your life. Secondly, if you have children and don't teach them to have good values—that they learn and incorporate—then the world (what they see on today's television and are exposed to online) will teach them. They will develop the values of television celebrities, their friends, teachers, professors, people in the workplace, and not yours.

M   O   V   E
Master   **Omit**   **Visualize**   **Execute**

What personal core values do you need to master to be more value-focused?

PERSONAL

_____

_____

_____

_____

_____

_____

PROFESSIONAL

_____

_____

_____

_____

_____

_____

What unwanted passengers do you need to omit?

PERSONAL

_____

_____

_____

_____

_____

_____

PROFESSIONAL

_____

_____

_____

_____

_____

_____

What action activities do you visualize to help sustain your personal core values?

PERSONAL

_____

_____

_____

_____

_____

_____

PROFESSIONAL

_____

_____

_____

_____

_____

_____

How will you execute your action plan?

PERSONAL

_____

_____

_____

_____

_____

_____

PROFESSIONAL

_____

_____

_____

_____

_____

_____

NOTES

SELF-TRANSFORMATION

Chapter 4

Watching for Falling Objects While Reconfiguring Your Choices

The decisions you make are a choice of values that reflect your life in every way.

—Alice Waters

We often confront our greatest fear at the crossroads of change. Fear makes our thoughts about how to move forward both complicated and overwhelming, whether we choose to turn right or left at the crossroads. In this chapter, I'll talk about a crossroads I encountered. The beauty about crossroads is there are choices to make. Regardless of the choices, there is something to learn, experience, and share.

Choice is a privilege in the sense that you can choose the opportunities you use to pursue your passion and purpose. Passion is the emotion behind what energizes and excites you. After cultivating my consciousness and series of consciousness moments in the late '90s, what energized and excited me was helping others learn what was necessary to become healthier, mind, body, and soul. In Chapter 1, I shared the actions of my passion and purpose. My present-day passion and purpose are centered more around helping others be better versions of themselves, and that happens by way of good choices.

THE TIME IS NOW. THE CHOICE IS YOURS.

On my varied journeys in life, I met so many people who have shared their aspirations and interests. Some of those aspirations and interests include:

- opening a retail store or restaurant,
- writing and publishing a book,
- launching a new career,

- completing your bachelor's degree,
- learning a new skill,
- increasing your knowledge about something,
- being selected as a contestant on a television game show,
- studying to become an actor,
- designing your own clothing brand,
- becoming a race car driver,
- traveling outside of your home state,
- taking your kids on a vacation to Washington, DC, to see the monuments,
- volunteering for a charitable organization,
- hiking the Grand Canyon,
- running a marathon,
- taking a fitness class at your local gym,
- creating a neighborhood association for your community,
- starting a book club at your company,
- owning a club,
- working as a barber,
- becoming a professional bartender, and
- being a farmer.

What about you? What thoughts energize you? What thoughts excite you? Share your specific thoughts here.

_____

_____

_____

_____

_____

YOUR ABILITY TO BELIEVE IS POWERFUL

If you have thoughts that limit your perspective about your choices—such as, *People like me don't get those opportunities* or *I don't have money to pursue that,* or *I don't have time because I care for my disabled child full time,* or *I have a medical condition that keeps me stuck in depression*—they are falling thoughts and can stifle the control you have to plan out your choices.

Our thoughts play a significant role in our life. We frequently believe the thoughts in our heads, but we don't have to. I want you to start thinking about analyzing, exploring, planning, prioritizing, and acting to identify and pursue your choices that will make your aspirations and interests a reality. The key is that you must put in the work. If you do, I know a happy and fulfilled life will follow. Then we can talk about ways you can make the same happen for those within your inner circle of influence.

YOUR CHOICES REQUIRE YOU TO THINK TRANSFORMATION

Life is full of opportunities to transform our lives. When we choose to start a new business, we must adjust and change to transform. Whether you choose to stay or leave a company, you must adjust and change to transform. Most often, we have to let go of something to gain something.

As a young adult, I reached a point in my life where I had to face a reality. I was at a series of crossroads, relying on food and alcohol to cover up, distract, and help me feel better. It covered up the things in my life that I didn't want to confront. Food provided a sense of power to help overcome my emotions, thoughts, feelings of disappointment, doubt, fear, resentment, and frustration. Food was something I could control. I could eat what I wanted, when I wanted, and how much I wanted. As one can imagine, I (1) overindulged and (2) made poor food choices that would have eventually led to major health problems and possibly early death. All the thoughts and feelings I tried to manage about my life eventually became too overwhelming, and I had to make some choices.

When you feel like your life is stuck in a traffic jam and you can't get out, making those small, manageable steps toward a goal you read about and hear people talk about seems overwhelming. You can't think clearly long enough to plot your plan to move your life forward, but if you think in terms of transforming your state of being, you can move. I know because I was tired of a revolving door of unhealthy relationships, always seeming to choose the wrong person to share my time and money. I was tired of always being in financial distress because of poor spending decisions, some because of those chosen relationships. I was tired of the thoughts surrounding something that happened to me and the haunting memories. I was fed up in too many aspects of my life. Once I properly analyzed the root causes and consequences, I said to myself, "Let the transformation process begin."

As I've mentioned before, there comes a time in all of our lives where we have to address the thoughts, feelings, and actions preventing us from living a life of peace and purpose. The self-analysis process helped me focus my attention on the barriers positioned throughout my road—things like work, the relationship, my finances, self-esteem, and a haunting past. Once I identified the barriers, I analyzed, explored, planned, prioritized, and acted on eliminating the barriers to move my life in a healthy, fulfilling, peaceful, and purposeful direction.

I decided to incorporate healthy lifestyle habits. One by one, I transformed my unhealthy habits through research and action. It's a part of being under construction. I eliminated unhealthy food choices, reduced my consumption of alcohol, and joined Bally's Total Fitness. My journey consisted of a lot of trial and error. In the process of it all, while walking on the treadmill and exercising on the StairMaster at Bally's, I contemplated trading in my Popeye's fried chicken for my homemade baked chicken, my Dr. Pepper for a bottle of water, my Snicker's bar for an apple, my Burger King Whopper for a homemade turkey burger, and my fries for a vegetable medley. As more research was conducted, doing so revealed significant hazards in the foods I ate, and that was over thirty years ago. If anything, the food products have gotten increasingly unhealthy.

I followed what later became known as my ten essential habits for living healthier during my years as a fitness coach. They were to be physically active, eat nutritious foods, eat breakfast, drink plenty of water, get adequate sleep, set goals for lifestyle modifications, get annual exams and screenings, avoid risky behaviors, examine your relationships, and live life with a purpose.

Everyone has choices as they think about their transformation, and so do you, regardless of your past and "right now." Whether your challenge is job-related, financial, health-related, or even related to criminal activity, you still have choices.

I love what Liletta shared with me about a choice she uses: "Every day, I choose to listen to the voice that tells me I'm amazing and that I can accomplish anything I decide to do. This isn't easy because there is another voice, at times the loudest voice, that tells me the opposite. So making the choice to silence that voice and pick the less popular voice in my head takes work and determination."

THE IMPACT ON YOUR PROFESSIONAL LIFE

Sometimes people can't identify and pursue their choices because of things that stifle their ability to think about and explore their options, such as the supervisor below, whose "right now" state of being fed up just might stifle his ability to choose and change his circumstances, thereby having a negative impact on his professional life.

- Billy, a supervisor for a manufacturing company, complains about his manager, saying, "My boss doesn't trust any of my decisions. He always gives flippant responses in front of my employees when I make a recommendation about a process improvement me and my team has talked about. And he privately makes decisions with my team about my division without including me. What's really disheartening is that he doesn't even know our processes in the assembly department. I'm so tired of feeling dismissed and devalued here. I need to figure out how to start my tea cakes business."

I know talking about and taking the steps to exit a "fed-up" state can be difficult, especially when it involves your job and dealing with a bad boss who scolds employees in front of others, who belittles and blames employees, who takes an employee's recommendation and presents the recommendation as their own instead of recognizing the employee who brought it forth, who threatens employees with talks of ending their employment, or who consistently lies about workplace matters.

The fact of the matter may be that you simply don't have the emotional, mental, or physical energy to do anything but stay in a situation that keeps you miserable, but you can't stay stuck in a "right now" that keeps you wallowing in misery. You have choices, and you have to ask yourself, "Now what?" so you can analyze and act on your choices to transform your situation and move forward.

Your situation may be comparable or different than Billy's, but the five steps below can help you be deliberate in identifying and pursuing your choices.

- Analyze the root cause of the issue driving your "fed-up" state or analyze the choices that can reduce or mitigate your "fed-up" state.

- Explore possible solutions that will help remove the issue or reduce the stress, depression, anger, sadness, or hopelessness caused by the issue.

- Plan a list of activities and tasks for each solution that can get you moving forward.

- Prioritize the solutions that will have a greater impact on gaining traction with your movement.

- Act on implementing the activities and tasks for the solutions selected.

In Billy's case, he could expend a lot of energy trying to figure out his manager's actions toward him, but he'd probably never get to the root cause. Only his manager can provide insight into why he treats Billy the way he does.

But what if the manager shares his insights? Billy may learn from his manager that he doesn't like him, doesn't think he's a good supervisor, doesn't think he's competent, or doesn't think he effectively leads his team. His boss's actions aren't illegal or a violation of company policy. They're just representative of a bad boss.

Billy does have choices. He can plan for his forever exit. He can use the steps to explore and pursue the creation of his tea cakes business.

DON'T SETTLE

The faith to understand and follow your destiny in the midst of unprecedented life challenges requires determination, sacrifice, strength, courage, and good judgment. Too often, we give up, throw in the towel, and settle for the status quo rather than exploring and pursuing our options to transform our situation. We lock ourselves into a routine and go through the motions, placing one foot in front of the other, trying to maintain stability among adversities that make their way into our lives.

I promise if you take the time to do the steps, you'll outline your options for removing the barriers and reconfiguring your path for forward movement. I shudder to think about where my life might be had I not taken the initial steps to MOVE.

I love what Tony shared about choices: "Having a choice means that I have the choice to stop and reevaluate my situation, regardless of the amount of pressure I may be experiencing. Too often, we set off on a journey and never stop to see whether we're going in the right direction and with the right supplies and people. Since the (weather) conditions may be changing, it may make sense to change our route or to stay in one place until the (weather) conditions change. I realized that I had a choice to terminate toxic relationships and to get rid of frenemies, including close relatives, in order to reach my destination."

Now is the time for change and transformation. Don't settle. The choice is yours. If you're ready to exercise your passion and purpose, continue reading. Be relentless in your pursuits. I remember hearing an NBA commentator say, "You can't teach relentless—relentless has to be in you." I sure hope it's in you.

Rest Stop Exercise #4

A BE to Remember: Be Reflective.

Reflection is necessary for growth and will reduce any inclination to repeat poor choices. It will ensure any mistakes we make are only new ones. Reflection helps us to stop saving the receipts of our past for the long haul and understand better when to discard them.

M O V E
Master   **Omit**   **Visualize**   **Execute**

What in your "right now" do you need to master to
position yourself to make better choices?

PERSONAL

_____

_____

_____

_____

_____

_____

PROFESSIONAL

_____

_____

_____

_____

_____

_____

What unwanted passengers do you need to omit?

PERSONAL

_____

_____

_____

_____

_____

_____

PROFESSIONAL

_____

_____

_____

_____

_____

_____

What action activities do you visualize to help you make better or enhanced choices?

PERSONAL

_____

_____

_____

_____

_____

_____

PROFESSIONAL

_____

_____

_____

_____

_____

_____

How will you execute your action plan?

PERSONAL

_____

_____

_____

_____

_____

_____

PROFESSIONAL

_____

_____

_____

_____

_____

_____

NOTES

Chapter 5

Being Prepared to Stop and Take Your Exit

Failure is the road you will travel to success.
Just be sure to take the correct exit.

—Tim Fargo

The beauty about the road of life is that for every on-ramp, there is an off-ramp. As you focus on transforming your life, you will have a series of ons and offs. I consider them as opportunities to be better. Sometimes you're unexpectedly forced off the road because of life's circumstances. In 2003, I was traveling on my healthy lifestyle road and unexpectedly was forced off due to mounting pain in my body. I ended up undergoing a series of blood work to pinpoint the source of severe aches and pains in my joints. The blood work indicated elevated levels of inflammation in my body. A couple years later, I was told by my rheumatologist that I was in remission after being treated for symptoms related to lupus.

For a friend of mine, Diane, the road traveled would end much differently. I met Diane in 2008 during a time we both served as half-marathon walk and run training coaches for the Crohn's and Colitis Foundation. In 2009, Diane was diagnosed with Lou Gehrig's disease. After Diane shared her diagnosis with her family and friends in 2009, I routinely checked on her via email. In March 2011, I received one of the last emails from Diane. She wrote, "B! I miss you!!! So great hearing from you and sorry I've been MIA. As for me…wish I had something positive to report. Symptoms have progressed except that the fasciculations (internal twitching) seemed less violent for a while. Maybe they are returning stronger again. I especially notice them after any sort of activity. Unfortunately, I can't run, bike, or swim anymore. I try to walk a couple times a week and do a little light resistance work, but it makes me very tired. My neck is especially weak, and I have difficulty holding up my head sometimes, especially if I bend over. But that is life, and life is hard sometimes."

Diane's email reminded me of how we can get too caught up with the problems, worries, and circumstances surrounding our involvement with things/people/dreams; so much so that a responsibility to pursue and fulfill our purpose can be hampered. In Diane's case, she had been blessed to have a remarkable life, participating in competitive sports and coaching competitive athletes. She had spent the majority of her life helping others live healthier, and she gave back to the community in so many ways. I would imagine Diane had navigated a series of on and off-ramps in her life.

While my medical situation was brief—for so many, it's not—I'm most grateful for what I experienced because it helped me to transform into a different and better person. It's unfortunate when something so drastic must happen in our lives to cause change. Nevertheless, for those times when I slip back, lose my focus, or get discouraged, it's Diane's last months on Earth that inspire me to do more. It also provides me with the perspective I need to get back on track. Diane passed in September 2011. You can read more about Diane's life here:

https://www.legacy.com/us/obituaries/elpasotimes/name/
diane-proud-obituary?pid=153669761.

DON'T STAY ON THE ROAD WHEN YOU NEED TO GET OFF

Our past can make us drive in circles, getting caught up on a loop of self-inflicted emotions that serve no purpose. The silver lining is that we can make our own off-ramp and move forward with passion, purpose, and intention.

Back in 2017, I was simply traveling on a road. I had done many things in my past, but I wasn't evolving in my "right now." Once again, I found myself going through the motions of life with no deliberate intention.

One day, I watched a television show where a veteran actor was talking about his acting journey. He shared that he was in pursuit of performing on Broadway, but because he didn't have a background in such, he needed to take acting lessons. A thought popped into my head about taking acting lessons. Acting is not something I had ever given considerable thought about. I did the research and found several companies offering classes in the Houston area. I found an exit from my current life road and selected a different road when I chose one of the companies and took acting lessons.

One of the things you learn in acting is the "Yes, and…" approach. Basically, it's a practice where you agree to let anything happen. You're presented with a scenario, and no matter what your fellow actors present to you, instead of opposing, belittling, or contradicting it, your job is to say, "Yes, and…" to add new information to it.

Below is an example of "Yes, and…":

Billy: I want to open a tea cakes business.

Friend: Yes, and you can create a business plan.

Billy: Yes, and I can conduct a SWOT analysis to identify my strengths, weaknesses, opportunities, and threats.

Friend: Yes, and you can assess how much capital you have available to invest.

Billy: Yes, and I determine if I want the business to be full time or part time.

Friend: Yes, and you can determine viability. Is there a market for your tea cakes?

Billy: Yes, and I can select a name for my business.

Friend: Yes, and you can register a domain name and secure social media profiles for your business.

Billy: Yes, and I can apply for an EIN with the IRS and local or state business licenses.

Friend: Yes, and you can research all of the necessary steps for setting up your business, ensuring you have sufficient funds, and planning for your business's business plan.

Billy: Yes, and I can hire you to help me with setting up the operation, marketing, and sustaining the business.

Now think about "Yes, and…" in our daily lives. If you apply it to your personal and professional life, you'll never reach an end to your "Now what?" This also allows you to use that exit ramp and take a new life road.

DREAM *BIG!* THEN *BELIEVE.*

To believe and act on your belief may require you to exit the road you're traveling. When we see businesses operating in our local communities, they represent people who had a dream, then analyzed, planned, believed, committed, and acted. They are working hard, being creative, being inventive, and happy exercising their choices to contribute to the economy and labor force of our country. You, too, can be one of the few who believe, have faith, and act on your dream. Don't be one of the people who don't think it's possible for them. More than likely, you're already making it possible for your employer. You're investing in their dream. Why not invest in yours?

Please keep in mind the probability that once you start talking about pursuing your dream and activating your plan, those around you will attempt to plant the seeds of doubt. The fact is that people with no dreams can't imagine yours. You simply can't listen to people who have never done anything outside of their comfort zone. Your vision of entrepreneurship—your vision of creativity, inventing, growth, and freedom to pursue your passion and your purpose is your journey to start. There will be risks, setbacks, and disappointments, but they all will lead to success during your series of trial and error.

Both Joyce and Tony are great examples of people who left their companies to pursue their dreams full time. It has been incredible for me to witness the pursuit of their passions. They work literally twenty-four hours/seven days a week—a lot of hard work and late hours mixed with fun and humor. I know they started with a plan. Even with a plan, no one knows how the journey will end. They knew they wanted to start, and they knew what they wanted to achieve.

In her book, *No Back Doors For Me*, Joyce states: "I would now be able to get the experience for which I had hoped to strengthen my portfolio and move into leadership within this organization or at least to equip myself for a leadership role in another company with a strong global base after a couple of years of development in this less expansive arena. Like all plans (even the good ones), they can be somewhat vulnerable to the environment around them."

I love to listen to people talk about public figures and the height of their accomplishments. They are admired. They are celebrated. People are fascinated by forward-facing success (what they see on the surface). Oftentimes, they don't consider that what they see is the result of years of hard work, late hours, setbacks, risks, and all of the stuff that contributes to success.

People in our communities who pursue their dreams and may never receive state or national recognition should be admired and celebrated too. They are not simply owners and operators of small businesses that add value to our country's economy. They're giving back to their local communities, to people in need, during crises and uncertainties. In the Houston, Texas, area, you can rest assured that when our local or nearby areas incur crisis and devastation, you'll hear the names of two people before you hear anyone else's. They are Frazier Othel Thompson III (known as Trae tha Truth), an American Rapper, and Jim "Mattress Mack" McIngvale, a Houston businessman. They are known as Houston's best-loved big names helping those in need. They thought big, believed in what they wanted, and changed their life road, which now allows them to improve the life roads of others.

KNOW WHEN IT'S TIME TO EXIT

If you don't love what you're doing, leave. I can say that the reason I planned my exit in my last capacity in the traditional workforce was because I no longer loved what I did. In the beginning, I loved doing something I had supervised but had never done myself on a full-time basis. After doing the same thing over and over, my love faded away. Maybe I felt I had regressed to just having a job. I no longer had the ability to have the sort of impact I had been accustomed to making in an organization. I now love the position I've created for myself that affords me a myriad of opportunities to help people and organizations be better—to be especially better in their professional life with regards to their customers (delivery of an experience with intention and a smile) and their workforce (employee engagement and team spirit). Impact!

Don't stay in a situation you don't love, you're not passionate about, and doesn't bring you joy! It's that simple. In my most recent "fed-up" state, it became evident that movement in the organization to a higher level was not a reality for me. So, I had two choices. I could stay and endure redundancy and exist with no voice, or I could plan my exit. No guessing about my decision is necessary. I planned my exit, and you can too!

In her book, *No More Back Doors*, Joyce talks about a conversation she had with a young woman: "Just yesterday, I helped a young woman of color put together a plan to navigate her next career move. After we were done, I said to her (and I would iterate the same to you), once you check off all these boxes, and they tell you that it is enough, and you still don't get the promotion, then make a decision to find a place where you will be celebrated versus tolerated! You owe it to yourself and to everyone around you to celebrate who you are, to be confident in your abilities, and to receive the rewards of your hard work. I know that there are companies out there that will offer you this, and if not, create your own because you are just that damn good!"

ANALYZE WHO AND WHAT NEEDS TO GO

The first thing is to analyze everything and everyone in your life, then omit the things and people who don't contribute to making you a better person. Yes, I know. We all see ourselves as good people, but we can always be better in our careers, financially, spiritually, emotionally, and physically. We can also be better as a spouse, partner, parent, sibling, relative, friend, coworker, church member, and community servant.

THE IMPACT OF MENTAL CLUTTER

Your mental state can affect your personal and professional endeavors in a variety of ways. A cluttered mind with undeserving thoughts, such as the following, will yield negative outcomes.

Personal

"I wish she'd get a real job that generates income."

"I shouldn't have loaned him that money."

"I should have waited to have a child."

"My kids are so selfish."

"I'll never get out of debt."

"I'll never lose weight."

"I do have daddy issues."

"Everyone else's birthday is a big deal except mine."

<u>Professional</u>

"I'll never get promoted at this company."

"The workload is too much."

"I'll never meet their expectations."

"My manager doesn't like me."

"My supervisor is trying to sabotage me."

"My colleagues are talking to management about me behind my back."

"My employees don't respect me."

Negative outcomes may be present by way of unfavorable disposition changes, a lack of energy, overeating or under-eating, insomnia, excessive sleeping, increase in medical mental aides, and/or excessive alcohol consumption. That's a lot of progressive damage and mental clutter.

What are your strongest negative thoughts? Write them down here. Be honest.

_____

_____

_____

_____

_____

What can you do to clear out the undeserving thoughts and limit the damage? Start by being silent and focus on self-transformation. Develop your PPP to focus your attention on clearing the mental debris on your pathways. To assist you with developing and completing your PPP, I've included PPP worksheets for your review and action, which are located in the Your Under-Construction Worksheets section of the book. They are designed to help you facilitate your MOVE.

Your process for clearing the pathway may lead to reduced stress, more energy, better eating, better sleep, reduced medical mental aides, and/or reduced alcoholic consumption.

Rest Stop Exercise #5

A BE to Remember: Be a Believer.

There will be times when your belief in yourself will be tested. You'll believe you need to stay because it's safer. You'll believe you need to stay because there are risks. No worries. You just need to make sure you plan for on and off "Now whats."

M O V E
Master   **Omit**   **Visualize**   **Execute**

What do you need to master to install a variety of on and off-ramps to achieve your goals? It simply means you need contingency plans.

PERSONAL

_____

_____

_____

_____

_____

_____

PROFESSIONAL

_____

_____

_____

_____

_____

_____

What unwanted passengers do you need to omit?

PERSONAL

_____

_____

_____

_____

_____

_____

PROFESSIONAL

_____

_____

_____

_____

_____

_____

What action activities do you visualize?

PERSONAL

_____

_____

_____

_____

_____

_____

_____

PROFESSIONAL

_____

_____

_____

_____

_____

_____

_____

How will you execute your action plan?

PERSONAL

_____

_____

_____

_____

_____

_____

PROFESSIONAL

_____

_____

_____

_____

_____

_____

NOTES

Chapter 6

Proceeding with Caution When Choosing Your Inner Circle

Choose your friends with caution; plan your future with purpose, and frame your life with faith.

—Thomas S. Monson

When we think about the purpose of a stop sign, it warns drivers to slow down and stop. We must yield the right-of-way to pedestrians and approaching vehicles before proceeding, and we should only proceed when it's safe to do so. When we think about the people we invite into our lives, there may come a time when we need to slow down and stop to assess the relationship before proceeding forward.

A few years ago, I was invited to become a member of a nonprofit organization. On paper, the nonprofit organization looked like an ideal fit for me. Its mission, along with its purpose to solve problems and enrich its community, was on target with my endeavors to make a difference in the community. Its actual use of donated funds was the stop sign that caused me to slow down. I would later stop and end my relationship with the organization because I realized it wouldn't be safe for me to proceed forward.

The beauty about the road of life is if you can get off course, no matter how often, and if you choose wisely, you can get the right directions from the right people in your life—people who know a better and safer way to travel.

THE RIGHT AND WRONG PEOPLE ON YOUR ROAD

The people who come into your life can change your life, so you want to make sure you choose your circle wisely regarding who'll travel with you on your road to transformation. These should be people who share the same values and who are transparent, ethical, and trustworthy. They will include personal (family and friends) and professional (teachers, mentors, coaches, current and former bosses, current and former coworkers, and industry colleagues) connections.

Think about your inner circle. Is there anyone on the inside holding you back? Let's say you want to take a class that interests you or you want to save some money. You might try to drive ahead, but they could be standing in the middle of the road and blocking your progression. They might believe taking a class will be a waste of your time. They could say you've got too many bills to start saving.

So how will you know who's who? You'll know. Just in case you need some examples, however, check out the chart below:

The Right People
Are ready for new experiences.
Take responsibility for their mishaps.
Apologize for any inconvenience that happens.
Are always publicly happy about the success of others.
Are always in learning mode to expand their knowledge and skills.
Welcomes hearing the perspective of others.
Will help you to determine solutions, apply solutions, make adjustments, assess the adjustments made, and pivot, if necessary.
Will support and believe in you no matter what.
Says: I love your idea. Let me know how I can help you. I want your endeavor to be successful.

The Wrong People
Are afraid of change.
Blame others for their own mistakes.
Never apologize even when they know they're wrong.
Privately wants to see others fail.
Knows everything.
Critical of others' perspective.

Says, "That'll never work. My friend did it and it didn't work for them."
Will support you only when they see you are popular and doing well on your pursuits.
Says, "Wow! There you go again! Always got something new going on. You're never satisfied."

Be sure you surround yourself with people who are moving. They will push you, celebrate you, and hold you accountable, but it doesn't stop there. You are also a participant in a repeated cycle of supporting, pushing, and celebrating them.

WHO YOU WANT ON YOUR "UNDER-CONSTRUCTION" PERSONAL PROJECT PLAN (PPP)

Your mother? Your father? Your sister? Your brother? Your mentor? Your barber? Your tax preparer? A childhood friend? A classmate? When you're on a road and moving to fulfill the objectives of your journey, you want to have that special group of people with whom you share, connect, and collaborate. They will see your vision, the things you want to achieve, and the difference you want to make. The people on your road don't see you as competition. They are not jealous of you. They are people who support and celebrate you and your achievements both privately and publicly.

They won't let you be distracted and unfocused on being a better version of yourself. They won't get you involved in illegal criminal activities. They won't condone your involvement in illegal criminal activities. They are not content with watching others evolve. They are focused and committed to evolving themselves.

The people alongside you while you're under construction will keep you grounded when success arrives. They will honestly and respectfully call you out when you start to get too caught up with your achievements and experiences. As my grandmother would say, they won't let you get "too big for your britches."

WHO YOU DON'T WANT ON YOUR "UNDER-CONSTRUCTION" PPP

I'm sure most of the people in your life are good people, but they may be stuck. The truth is that you can't move forward surrounded by stuck people. They may be good for those times when you simply want to travel, celebrate, and have a good time, but don't make hanging around them a habit. If you hang around them too long, you'll notice things you need to be guarded about.

Be guarded with people who always share their interests and ideas, but they have not done anything to advance their interests and ideas. They are stuck, and listening to the perspective of a stuck person will impair the pursuit of your vision.

Be guarded with people who discount or change the subject when you're sharing your interests or ideas about something. They are stifling, and listening to the perspective of a stifling person will impair the pursuit of your vision.

Be guarded with people who seemingly always bring up your past acts and mistakes during the times you're sharing your interests or ideas—past acts and mistakes that may not be flattering. They are inhibitors, and listening to the perspective of an inhibitor will impair the pursuit of your vision.

Be guarded with people who are naysayers. They will say, "That can't be done," "That's not going to work," "John Doe tried it, and it didn't work out," "You're crazy," and "You've got a good thing going with your employer." They are doubters, and listening to the perspective of a doubter will impair the pursuit of your vision.

If you encounter any of these reactions to your ideas, aspirations, and pursuits, simply smile and say, "Thank you for listening to my idea. I was looking for another point of view. You've given me something to think about," then keep it moving. At this point in life, you probably know with whom in your circle you can share your dreams, ideas, aspirations, and pursuits.

The wrong people in your life will contribute to your reckless decisions, destructive lifestyle behaviors, unhealthy relationships, drug addiction, excessive alcohol consumption, and impulsive spending habits.

When I asked Ken, Daniel, Liletta, and Tony about their inner circle, they shared the following:

- **Ken:** In most cases, you cannot control who is in your inner circle, especially when it comes to family and coworkers. In any case, your inner circle will include people who do not share your interests. I just think it is important that you try to exclude those who do not share your moral values and those who attempt to preclude you from reaching the goals that you set for yourself.

- **Daniel:** Having the right people in my inner circle is key to my success. When I started my real estate business, I met other realtors that gave me advice. They helped me with contract decisions, and as I learned the business, I was able to help them as well. In starting my trucking business, I talked to many of my friends that are in the business, and I talked to other people in the business.

- **Liletta:** In my opinion, your inner circle will be diverse and ever-changing. Who you have the closest to you will depend on what you are trying to accomplish. In general, I've found that you need a yes-person—someone who will always encourage you that you can do it! But you also need a nah-sis person. This is a person that will let you know if you are just simply about to do something that is going to harm you either personally or professionally. Also, you need someone that is business savvy, along with someone that is strong in the areas you aren't.

- **Tony:** In hindsight, the people in my inner circle share three common characteristics. First, we ask how we can help the other person instead of looking at what the other person can do for us. Second, we can be vulnerable and express our fears without feeling weak. Third, we don't discourage one another. Instead, we focus on finding solutions to problems.

  Running marathons helped me expand my physical and mental comfort zones. By traveling to all fifty states and seven continents, I had experiences that many people only read about or watch on video. Surround yourself with caring friends who will challenge you to move outside of your comfort zone. Never be too old to learn from others.

THE IMPACT ON YOUR PROFESSIONAL LIFE

Let's say you love the career field you're working and your organization. The decision-makers in your company raved about your ability to develop, innovate, and produce. They consider you a valued asset and a contributor to the growth of the organization. It's understandable why you have excelled. You have diligently worked on your personal and professional development, which includes a diverse inner circle.

Now you're poised to move on to the next level, but are you ready to be the next leader in your organization, some other organization, or your own organization? Are you ready for the roles associated with being a leader? Roles like:

- visionary,
- influencer,
- learner,
- strategist,
- decision-maker,
- change-agent,
- motivator,
- coach,
- mentor, and
- role model.

Are you ready for the team of people within your circle of influence and responsibility who will be front and center, ready to follow you?

Too often, leaders don't take the time to meet the moment, to study the diversity of their team members, or to unite team members. Could it be because their inner circle is limited? Their inner circle consists of people who think, feel, and act as they do, so when it comes to leading a team (formally or informally), their messaging may be off.

Research has shown that the use of messaging apps, text, and social media to "communicate" rather than calling or walking down the hall or to a person's desk is having a counter effect. The technology that was supposed to connect us is disconnecting us. Our technological interactions have resulted in less meaningful dialogue and have driven us away from social in-person connections.

How can meaningful dialogue be reinstituted? It's simple. Be the person who is focused on social and emotional connections. Organizations are screaming "inclusion." They are focused on having a diverse workplace where everyone feels connected, so you lead connective actions by inviting others regardless of age, race, national origin, sex, or disability to be a part of a workplace circle. You can be the person who visibly and authentically recognizes collaborative successes, celebrates the career changes of others, and works to unite your workplace.

It'll be up to you as the leader (by title or influence) to set the tone for the work environment. I've heard supervisors talk about how praising employees is not what they do—they do not have the time or the energy. It further amazes me when I hear a leader make comments like the following:

"I'm not touchy-feely."

"I'm just not a warm-fuzzy sort of person."

"I don't have time to stroke an employee's ego."

"I don't have time to dish out praise and accolades."

I say, "Shame on that leader." Being a successful leader requires you to be a people person. Always remember that the occasional pat on the back, "job well done" comment, and surprise breakfast treats aid in creating a team of employees who love and are devoted to the company. Also, working with your human resources department to create a good performance management program can be a lot of help when showing your appreciation and recognizing employees.

Employees are observant of their leaders—their personality, treatment of employees, and consistency of policy application. If there is conflict among your team, then you—as the leader—may not be doing all you can to model and convey trust, respect, empathy, appreciation, and celebration of the unique skills and talents of your team members.

Today's companies are filled with more unhappy and unfulfilled employees than with happy and fulfilled employees. You just may be one of those unhappy and unfulfilled employees. Employees are the life or death of any company. If your employees are happy and fulfilled, then your customers are happy and satisfied. Employees do have the power to make or break your company's reputation. Unhappy and unfulfilled employees can cause a company to lose millions in revenue and shut its doors for good.

The workplace can be a source of unhappiness and unfulfillment. Work can impact the personal life, and the personal life can influence the workplace. It is the responsibility of the supervisor to make sure the workplace is the employee's place of refuge.

Just as I have through the years, I know you've overheard workplace conversations about employees that are comparable to the examples cited below:

- [Name of employee] just needs a spouse. That's why he/she is so mean and crappy. No one can work with him/her.
- [Name of employee] is so controlling and judgmental.
- [Name of employee] gets so emotional about everything.
- [Name of employee] walks in the door angry every morning.
- [Name of employee] is always comparing and in competition with everyone.
- [Name of employee] always looks so sad.
- [Name of employee] stresses out about everything.
- [Name of employee] contradicts everything.
- [Name of employee] always presents the worst-case scenario.
- [Name of employee] never has any money to contribute to the birthday fund.
- [Name of employee] must be doing drugs or drinking alcohol in the restroom. It seems like he/she is going in there every five minutes with a bag.
- [Name of employee] falls asleep during every team meeting.

YOUR WORKPLACE INNER CIRCLE

A team can only be better and successful together, and some key elements that facilitate this are acknowledgments, inclusion, praises, and celebrations. There is the likelihood of some disagreements, differing of opinions, and internal conflicts occurring, but at the end of the day, it's about decency, respect, collaboration, support, and results.

As an HR consultant, I hear countless stories of employees who feel left out and over-looked when it comes to inclusion—involvement in constructive conversations and collaborative solutions. Sometimes, exclusion may be a consequence of conscious and unconscious bias. That's why I consistently endeavor to keep my finger on the pulse during our never-ending discussions about politics, economics, social justice, criminal justice, healthcare, and the other various areas of people's concerns.

It's highly likely that you, your employees, and your team members have opinions about the never-ending discussions resulting in conscious and unconscious biases. Those opinions and biases will likely seep into the workplace.

It's important to better understand the individual and team dynamics in work environments that include people from diverse communities, upbringings, experiences, opinions, and perspectives. This focal point helps me to better guide and support my clients with their diversity and inclusion initiatives, but it's always amazing to me—as someone who typically has an inside track—to see how much we all have in common when we sit at the same tables and interact with one another, together.

The bottom line is everyone in the workplace—regardless of race, national origin, age, sex, gender, religion, and political affiliations—wants the same thing. That is to be respected and treated fairly and equally. You and your supervisor or manager, as leaders, have a lot to do with communicating so everyone feels respected, connected, and valued as a team member, which happens by way of messaging. Good communication and dialogue cultivate a shared vision and participation in fostering creativity, innovation, and productivity.

I encourage you to take the time to learn about your team members. Find commonalities and shared interests because the more you know about someone within your inner circle at work, the more you understand them. It may help you reevaluate and/or omit any biases you might have. Discussing those commonalities and shared interests help team members get to know each other better, which can facilitate problem-solving, decision-making, collaboration, support, improved morale, and increased productivity in the workplace.

You and your team members will come into the workplace with baggage (past and present) because all of us, at some point, will experience some degree of life's challenges. Through whatever personal challenges you may be experiencing, the expectation with your employer is that you and your team members remain focused on your job. It's important to mention that your customers, clients, and patrons will be diverse, and they, too, will walk through your doors while dealing with life's challenges.

By no means do you ever want to overshare your personal life with your coworkers/team members, and proceed with caution with what you do share in the workplace. A good rule of thumb is to never share anything you don't mind being repeated. Always avoid sharing information about your finances, health problems, relationships, marriage, kids, religion, political affiliation, family drama, social activities (partying and drinking), or negative feelings about the boss, an employee, team member, client, or customer.

If your goal is to advance in your organization or some other organization, you never want to disclose information that may be considered when decisions about you are being made. You never want to risk the person you shared the information with slipping up and sharing information you intended to be confidential with someone else.

When I talk about commonalities and shared interests in your inner circle, I'm referring to activities that can positively connect team members. The fact is you spend more hours with your employees, coworkers, and team members than with your family, so it's not unusual to want to know something about them. Activities to do together could be things like training for a marathon, taking a cooking class, attending a sporting event, or learning a new language. Relatable people can create collaborative, meaningful, memorable, and productive work environments. They can better listen, share, connect, and care.

DEFINITE DON'TS

Never joke about or make references related to age in the workplace (i.e., "You're too old to work here," or "When are you going to retire?"). Never joke about or make references to race, color, or gender in the workplace. Never make comments like "You know you're special." A person who overhears the comment may take offense to the comment, believing you are referencing a person with a disability. Never joke about the weight or appearance of employees in the workplace. "She shouldn't have worn those skinny jeans on casual day."

As a leader, you can't get too comfortable with your employees. Doing so will inevitably lead to comfortable comments with your employees, which will inevitably lead you to overlook or dismiss the comfortable comments of others—your employees, for instance. For one person, a comment may be a joke, but for another, it may be offensive.

Too often, leaders overlook or dismiss the comments of employees. I remember a time investigating a case where an employee would make comments while laughing like, "You didn't learn technology back in your day. I know it's frustrating. When are you going to retire?" Or "Late night? You looking mighty drunk limping around here, friend." Or "Quit playing and do your work. Don't be like the other Black people." Well, the limping person had a disability that had flared up.

Don't be too sensitive to hear a straight-forwarded perspective. People oftentimes get too caught in the tone and tenor to hear the message. If the people in your life do not aid and abet you to a higher level, *omit*! Don't miss the signs.

If your employee or team member comes to you and says, "I didn't feel supported by you during the meeting." Don't respond by saying, "You're being sensitive." "Don't be so dramatic." Don't dismiss the employee's feelings. If you don't agree with the employee's feeling, you want to sit down to talk and show empathy and curiosity.

Rest Stop Exercise #6

A BE to Remember: Be Cautious.

The people in your inner circle can make or break you. You want to make sure you add people to your path who can facilitate your growth. You want to make sure you choose wisely.

M   **O**   **V**   **E**

Master   **Omit**   **Visualize**   **Execute**

What in your "right now" do you need to master the avenues
you'll take to add the right people to your inner circle?

PERSONAL

_____

_____

_____

_____

_____

_____

PROFESSIONAL

_____

_____

_____

_____

_____

_____

What unwanted passengers do you need to omit?

PERSONAL

PROFESSIONAL

What action activities do you visualize to make better people choices?

PERSONAL

_____

_____

_____

_____

_____

_____

PROFESSIONAL

_____

_____

_____

_____

_____

How will you execute your action plan?

PERSONAL

_____

_____

_____

_____

_____

_____

PROFESSIONAL

_____

_____

_____

_____

_____

_____

NOTES

SELF-EVOLUTION

Chapter 7

Reducing Your Speed to Show Your Gratitude

We must find time to stop and thank the people who make a difference in our lives.

—John F. Kennedy

Whether you're running your first or twentieth marathon, it will be a life-changing experience running 26.2 miles on the streets, roads, highways, and byways of a city or town in ideal, cold, warm, or hot weather conditions. At least, that's been my experience. Even if I don't feel my best or I'm concerned about a nagging injury, my goal is to enjoy the experience and get through the event.

Regardless of any circumstances, when it's race day, I know it's going to be something special. I've trained for months doing speed work and hill training. I'm more committed to my bodywork and mat Pilates class at the gym. I've focused for months on my nutrition, tried new energy products, and eliminated food products. I've purchased at least two pairs of running shoes during the proceeding months for training and race day. I've consistently read a variety of resources about running, training, and nutrition for advice and recommendations that will hopefully facilitate optimal training and performance conditions.

On race day, I'm anxious. I'm with a group of my running friends, but I'm anxious. If it's an out-of-town race, I'm thinking about if I walked too much doing sightseeing and whether my legs will get tired early on in the race. I'm thinking about if what I ate the days before or morning of will impact my performance, wondering if/when my stomach will start to act up. Depending on the time of year, I'm wondering how the weather may impact my performance on the course and my finish time.

At the start line, the expected happens. I've got to exit the starting area and find a portable toilet to relieve the contents of my upset stomach. It seems to never fail.

With all I'll experience, there are three groups I'll look forward to seeing on the course—the volunteers, the law enforcement officers, and the spectators. They all provide the support and encouragement the runners will need during the 26.1 miles of walking, jogging, running, and a combination thereof.

When I finally start running, I look forward to the volunteers. I know the course will be lined with many of them handing us products like water, the selected sports drink, or a piece of fruit or sports bar. They will yell out words of support and encourage-ment like, "You're looking strong," "Great job," "You're almost there," "You've got one mile left," or "You've got this," in response to an approaching hill. If my name is on my running bibs, I will more than likely hear someone say, "Go, Coach Collins!" Their never-ending smiles and cheers are a welcome sight, especially when I'm on the downside of a hill or approaching the end. They never fail to add to the excitement as I pass by.

Law enforcement personnel will smile as we're passing, and some may even utter words of encouragement. I'm simply grateful they're out there protecting and ensur-ing our safety as we run on streets, roads, highways—whatever the terrain. The spec-tators are great as they cheer their hearts out for us. I'm grateful for them too.

One of the things I look forward to doing is saying "thank you." I always slow down and say thank you as I'm running past the volunteers. I know the individuals have signed up to volunteer. They were given an assignment (from event set-up, parking, packet pick-up, gear check, hydration station, safety team, cheer team, finish line, and the award ceremony to the tear down and clean up). They spend countless hours—working several shifts—to fulfill their assignments. I don't know the volunteers or why they're volunteering, but I'm grateful for their presence and want them to know it.

My running friends know this is one of the things I do during a race. They will tease me, saying, "You wear yourself out thanking everyone you pass." I know I'm not the only runner who does it, as I'll hear other random runners yelling out their thanks as well.

I love this quote by Sterling K. Brown: "Always have an attitude of gratitude." To have an attitude of gratitude regardless of the who, what, why, and when is essential to being a better version of ourselves, but life's journey is different for all of us. You may find yourself weighed down by the past and present perils of life, and you simply don't have an attitude of gratitude mindset.

Some find it difficult to have a grateful attitude when contending with painful memo-ries and "right now" situations like:

- the tragic death of a parent that left the family distraught emotionally, men-tally, physically, and financially;

- an abusive parent that left the family scarred emotionally, mentally, physically, and financially;

- a parent with an alcohol, legal or prescription drugs, gambling, food, spending, or social media addiction that left the family damaged emotionally, mentally, physically, and financially;

- witnessing the death of a family member from suicide;

- being raped or molested as a youth;

- being bussed from the hood to a school where the kids who were of a higher economic status bullied you because of your family's economic status;

- being placed in the juvenile justice system as a youth; or

- being mistreated by a coworker.

Their "right now" attitude of gratitude simply may not exist because of the consumption of thoughts and feelings surrounding their pain. A past that consists of hurt, pain, and tragedy cannot be overcome without the appropriate attention, but we can enter a place where we choose to seek the good amid the bad. When we do, some amazing things can happen.

WHAT WOULD YOU DO? SHOW GRATITUDE?

One of my favorite TV shows is *What Would You Do?* I love this show and its concept of using hidden cameras and actors to show how everyday people respond when they are confronted with a problem that requires them to take action. The everyday people will either take action by rendering an opinion or showing their disapproval, or they may simply walk away and mind their own business. Behind the scenes, the host observes actions and comments of everyday people, which on certain episodes, have gotten heated when the scenarios involve someone's poor treatment. In all instances, you'll see an act of gratitude.

When you consider the following, what would you do?

- The person who sees you approaching an entrance and holds the door open for you.

- The person in the grocery line who has twenty items, sees you with three, and allows you to go ahead of them.

- The driver who sees you at a standstill at an intersection trying to enter onto a street and allows you to enter.

- The neighbor who sees your trashcan at your curb for several days, figures you're out of town, and walks over to roll your trashcan into your yard.

- The friend who remembers you have a medical appointment and sends you a word of prayer and well wishes via a text message.

- The coworker who knows you had a relative to pass away and gives you a sympathy card.

I'm hopeful that when you experience comparable random acts of kindness from others, they will transform your outlook about the things in your life. Your "Now what?" can be really simple. You simply decide to be grateful in spite of your past and present circumstances, no matter what burdens you may be carrying. You can be grateful, and in answer to the question of what you would do, you show your gratefulness to others. So, what does your gratefulness look like? For starters, you simply smile, acknowledge, and say, "Thank you," to the person either verbally or in writing.

In Chapter 2, I talked about the contentment journal that my running friend, Tracy, gave me, and I told how the journal helped to address the things stifling my present-day "Now what?" As I think about the benefits of the journal, I'd like to encourage you to start keeping a gratitude journal. Your gratitude journal can simply be you using the notepad app on your cellular telephone, setting up a Word document on your computer, a paper notepad, or some other tool to record each day what you're grateful for. Your entry can be as simple as stating, "I'm grateful I woke up." You can write as many lines as you want and express what you're grateful for at the beginning or end of your day. Even if you're unhappy or burdened about someone or something in your life, there's always a reason to be grateful. It's helpful to get in the habit of acknowledging those reasons, so as you consider your "Now what?" in life, you'll do so with a different state of mind.

WHAT YOU DO IMPACTS YOUR PARENTAL ROLE

In Chapter 3, I talked about gratitude, which is being appreciative for what you receive, whether tangible or intangible. I talked about the development of personal core values, the role of a parent, and those in parental roles. When kids are taught to be grateful at an early age, that gratefulness transcends into adult life (with their family and friends, in their work environments, and in their communities), but you can only effectively teach your child about this important personal core value when you're not caught up in your "fed-up" state.

As I listen to today's parents and their conversations about their child, there is usually an emphasis on how well their kid is doing academically in school (good grades), their child's various extracurricular activities, where they are considering applying to college and their college prospects, SAT scores, acceptance to an academic summer program at a prominent university, and/or acceptance to a good university with a scholarship. They are excited parents, and rightfully so, but there's so much sharing about their child's giftedness with little showing of their gratefulness.

The little showing of gratitude comes into play when the child receives a gift or some token of congratulations, and there is no returned expression of thanks, no telephone call, no text message, and no thank-you card. This same child grows up to be an adult, graduating from college, getting a new home, getting married, having a baby, or experiencing some other milestone occasion. There is an expectation of a gift of some sort, but because this new adult hasn't been taught as a child how to show gratitude, there is a new generation lacking in showing it.

THE SOCIETY IMPACT

Recently, I saw a social media post of a friend. The friend asked the question, "Does anyone say 'thank you' or 'excuse me' anymore?" As you can imagine, the post received several responses. I responded, "Good manners have been on the decline for a while." Someone else responded, "The older folks are just as rude as the younger ones."

For the past few years, there have been expanded conversations about privilege and entitlement. Let's think about privilege and entitlement from a different perspective. Initially, I thought that parents and individuals with parental responsibility are raising a generation of kids who expect to receive from others without having to show their gratitude. The truth is, adults have seemingly reached a conclusion that there's no need to show gratitude. As a consequence, our younger generation in society are subject to follow suit.

A GOOD RULE OF THUMB

When you're grateful for what someone has done for you, you should be excited to let them know. It doesn't matter if they are a family member, friend of the family, friend of a friend, or foe. I remember a conversation I had with a former coworker many years ago. She was the mother always bringing her kid's fundraising activities to work. She sold cookies, popcorn, candy, houseware products—you name it, she brought it to work to sell. I remember us having a conversation one day about her having her ten-year-old child send thank-you notes to all of the purchasers.

Long after the mother and I no longer worked together, I would receive an invitation for those milestone graduations and when the child became an adult and entered the military. Every time I sent the child/young adult a gift, I received a handwritten thank-you note—a perfect example of a parent who taught her child the importance of showing his gratefulness.

One of my favorite things to do is write while eating breakfast and drinking coffee at a favorite restaurant. During one of my restaurant visits, I engaged in a conversation with a gentleman that included current events—the rise in road rage, domestic violence, the need for property tax reform, and reforming the statutes governing homeowners' associations (HOAs). As we spoke, the gentleman shared a story about a neighbor. He talked about the neighbor never having their yard maintained (cut, trimmed, and edged), and after months of no attention, the yard was a hot mess. He described how the limbs on the trees were almost hanging to the ground. He talked about how he and another neighbor cut the neighbor's yard and the limbs on the tree.

I could tell he was still irritated that the neighbor never said, "Thank you." He talked about seeing the neighbor outside one day. He asked the neighbor, "Did you see your lawn cut and trees trimmed?" He recounted that the neighbor said, "Oh yeah. Thank you." According to the man, the neighbor knew who had cut the lawn and trimmed the trees, but he never even bothered to thank him until prompted to do so.

As someone who has consistently maintains my own lawn, I would have been ecstatic that someone cut my lawn and trimmed my trees for free. I would never want to leave an impression of ingratitude on someone's mind. The gentleman who shared the story with me never said it, but I think he and the other neighbor would probably think twice before helping their neighbor again. The point is to never miss or dismiss an opportunity to say "thank you" when a random or purposeful act of kindness is bestowed upon you.

A few years ago, an old friend of mine ensured I received an invitation to her adult child's wedding. She sent me a private message through Facebook to ensure I had received the invitation and inquire if I would attend. The wedding was in another state, and I was unable to attend in person. I shipped a wedding gift to the newlyweds. After about three months, I hadn't received any indication that the wedding gift was received. I contacted my friend to inquire about the receipt of the gift. She indicated that the gift was received. I shared with her that the newlyweds hadn't acknowledged receipt of the gift. There was silence, and I thought, "*Wow!* How ungrateful." I thought about how the monies spent on the gift and shipping could have been donated or given to someone in need. Or toward a new pair of running shoes.

Being grateful is one of those values that truly starts at home. At the time of writing this book, both my parents are alive. I am so grateful for the value of gratitude they taught me. My mom has an old friend who will send me $5 or $10 each year for my birthday. Even in my ripe older age, my mother will say, "Did you call or send sis a thank-you card?" She doesn't have to remind me, but she does. I remember telling a friend of mine that I didn't get a thank-you card from her daughter after attending a baby shower. My friend of many years responded, "I don't know why she didn't send out thank-you cards." My thought was maybe she (my friend) should have encouraged her daughter to send them. I was taught that no matter how small or large you think about something, if the person thought enough of you to gift you something (money or time), then you need to send a proper thank you. Simply put: The person didn't have to do it.

If you are a parent or someone with parental responsibilities, it's up to you to help your child(ren) explore their options for taking an old-school, back-to-basics approach to show their gratitude. Doing so will aid them in influencing and building not only personal relationships but their professional relationships. Below are a few sampling acts of gratitude:

- Send a personalized follow-up email.
- Send a handwritten thank-you note.
- Send a birthday message to someone who wouldn't expect you to do so.
- Send a holiday greeting to a family member.

During the time Condoleezza Rice was the United States secretary of state, I remember my mother sharing she had sent her (Condoleezza Rice) a birthday card for her birthday. Some months later, my mother shared that she received a thank-you note from then-President George W. Bush. Even though the thank-you note was from the president, my mother was surprised about having received a thank-you card. So, when someone I know tells me, "He/she has been busy with schoolwork" or "I don't know why he/she hasn't sent those thank-you cards," I say, "Don't talk to me about privilege or entitlement."

The bottom line: It's important to teach your child to never delay, miss, or dismiss an opportunity to show their gratitude. Doing so can be as simple as sending a personalized text message, email, or buying a pack of thank-you cards from Walmart. A pack of forty-eight to sixty cards can range anywhere from $6.99 to $16.99 in price. They are much cheaper at your local dollar store. Walmart and other stores have specialty greeting cards for thanks related to graduation, wedding, wedding party, bridal shower, baby shower, gender reveal, sympathy, Christmas, and other occasions for which you or your child may receive a gift. Handwriting a personalized message is my favorite, then I send the card the old-fashioned way through the US postal system. Regardless of whether it's an acknowledgment worthy of a "thank you" or a gift value at $5, $50, or $500, you're teaching your child to be consistently grateful for anything someone gives them. It's the gift that keeps on giving—the gift of gratitude.

Who in your life do you need to send a thank-you card/note? Write down the name and words of thanks on a notecard or piece of paper, and share it either face-to-face, by US mail, email, or text message.

_____

_____

_____

_____

_____

THE IMPACT ON YOUR PROFESSIONAL LIFE

Gratitude is one family value that will serve you well and make a positive impact on your work environment. Consider for a moment that you are not the most talented or skillful employee on your work team, but you've exhibited a grateful heart. You are exceptional at engaging, reaching, and influencing others. Showing gratitude is a personal core value that has positioned you as the best fit for upward mobility in the organization.

We all can always be better at expanding our acts of gratitude—our appreciation—especially in the workplace. Gratitude is not limited to a supervisor communicating appreciation to a team member. Gratitude can be communicated in any direction, such as coworker to coworker and team member to team member. Whether you're the owner of a company or leader/manager/supervisor within an organization who wants to take your business/organization to the next level, motivating your employees through authentic appreciation is a key element for doing so. You must first seek to understand how to communicate appreciation to each individual employee and/or member of your team in a meaningful way.

Understanding what's meaningful to your employees requires direct communication. When was the last time you were shown or showed your appreciation to a coworker/team member? Why are these gratitude actions so important? Because of your business's five Rs. When you genuinely express your gratitude in the workplace, its impact will be significant. Check out the five Rs below:

- **Relationships.** It all starts with cultivating healthy relationships in the workplace. Your acts of gratitude toward all employees on your team will make them feel valued and appreciated for their contributions and delivery of products and services.
- **Retention.** These same employees will go above and beyond to deliver be-

haviors of value and appreciation to your customers, keeping your customers returning to purchase products and services offered by your company.

- **Referrals.** Your customers are so happy about the experience they've received from your employees' delivery of products and services; they are eager to share the name of your company and provide information about its offerings with others.

- **Reputation.** Because of your employees' actions and your faithful customers, your company has a solid reputation regarding the customer experience and its products and services.

- **Revenue.** The impact of healthy relationships, customer retention, and referrals are evident by increased sales and profits for your company.

I hear it over and over again from the employee who feels mistreated and unappreciated. "My company treats its employees poorly." "My manager never shows any appreciation for my hard work." "My company offers no upskilling, reskilling, or retraining. Nor opportunities for advancement." In 2021, there were a lot of articles published with the title starting off with "The Great Resignation." The articles focused on the reasons why a large percentage of employees were voluntarily leaving their jobs. There were a number of reasons given from people having a shift in priorities as a result of the 2020 pandemic to changing professions, starting a business, and making decisions based on home/family life. But one of the primary reasons was because of the treatment of employees. If you didn't say it, I'm sure you heard someone say one or more of the following:

- "I don't have to put up with this crap."
- "My manager never says thank you for all the extra work I do."
- "I haven't had a pay increase in forever."
- "They won't consider flexible work schedules. My cousin's organization offers telework and remote work options for eligible employees."
- "There are no reward systems in place."
- "They're always making changes, and we're always the last to know."
- "The company has never offered me any training opportunities to increase my knowledge and enhance my skills."
- "The same people keep getting promoted."

If you don't treat employees well, you work them hard, you don't reward them, and you don't show your appreciation toward them, they will stay because they believe they have no other options. But they will leave at the first opportunity.

If you're someone who aspires to be a leader in an organization, you must lead with a grateful heart. Employees want to know they are appreciated for their contributions to the organization/team, but appreciation is not a one-size-fits-all kind of thing. If it's important to you, then you'll explore your options for showing your appreciation—such as treating them with respect and offering them opportunities to grow with your organization, investing in training and creating opportunities for your employees to enhance skills and learn new skills, or creating programs that foster work/life balance. Engaged leaders know about their employees' career aspirations and targets. You may learn from your employee that they are interested in going back to school to finish their college degree. Working a split-shift schedule may be the only way they can work and fulfill the educational requirements.

So, what should be the first steps of an engaged leader? Sit down with your employees and ask them what motivates them. Ask them questions like:

> What do you love about your job?
>
> Do you prefer to work independently or to work in a group collaborating with others?
>
> What do you like to do outside of work?

You may find out the employee wants to work in a different position. You may find out the employee is passionate about an area in which he/she would be more valuable to the organization. You may find out the employee prefers to work independently. You may find out the employee runs in 5K races, bakes and sells cookies, goes fishing on the weekends, plans party events, etcetera. These types of questions are key to motivating and understanding what's important to your employees.

Some companies use survey tools easily accessible online that allow employees to describe a time they felt appreciated for their job performance. This will provide insight on how to make sure all of your employees receive consistent and personalized recognition in ways that make them feel appreciated. You'll probably find that employees vary between wanting public and private recognition. The insight you gain will enable you to implement different ways to show appreciation to individual employees in the way they will most appreciate. An employee preferring private recognition, for example, may have the opposite reaction than what you expect when praising them publicly.

Engaged leaders are focused on rewarding and recognizing their employees. Verbal recognition can be most effective. Whether in-person or via one of the video conferencing tools, you provide specific and meaningful recognition conversations. Below is an example of a recognition conversation:

- This is what you did.
- This is why it was impactful.

- How can you expand your actions to further the impact?
- How can I better support you as a partner for future wins?
- Do you mind if I share a suggestion with you?

Other ways you can show your appreciation include a handwritten note or an email. Or there may be an opportunity to give your employee a $5.00 coffee or gas card to express your thanks. I been in environments where a platter of donuts and pastries are provided for celebratory occasions. Well, the platter is fine until most of your team members become health conscious. Nevertheless, it's the little things on a daily basis that leave employees feeling important. The choice is yours. Just don't miss your opportunities to show your appreciation.

When communicating face-to-face appreciation, remember the following:

- Be timely.
- Be appropriate with being public or private.
- Be genuine.
- Be specific.
- Be inclusive.

In this scenario inclusive means recognizing and showing your employee appreciation in front of your boss. Let's say your employee delivered a great customer experience, worked a double shift, performed the work of an absent employee, or streamlined a process. Praise your employee in front of your boss. Doing so is a great way to foster value, build trust, strengthen the relationship, and ensure a better employee experience.

Check out this example: "Mary, thank you very much for helping me ensure the accuracy of the custodial products yesterday. I really appreciate you staying after hours to make sure the products were ready for shipment first thing this morning. I couldn't have done it without you!"

Gratitude for others will have a long-lasting and positive impact on professional relationships and will make for a healthier work environment.

Tips to remember:

- Don't overdo appreciation.
- Don't compliment just to be complimenting.
- Don't compliment just because you think it's what the person wants or needs to hear.

- Don't compliment on someone else's behalf. Avoid meaningless, inflated language.

As you expand your acts of gratitude, it's important to understand the relationship between gratitude, employee engagement, job performance, and organizational goals. Employees who feel appreciated and valued are more engaged. If they are more engaged, they will eagerly show up to work and be committed to working hard to achieve organizational goals.

Two simple words—thank you—with a lot of power when genuinely communicated will build, strengthen, and foster positive workplace connections.

DON'T FORGET TO EXPLORE AND EXPAND APPRECIATION ACTS FOR CUSTOMERS

Explore your options for taking an old-school, back-to-basics approach to customer appreciation. Doing so will influence and build customer loyalty and support, contributing to the next level of organizational growth. You can do things such as:

- send personalized follow-up emails to your customers,
- include a handwritten thank-you note with your customer's order,
- send a birthday message to your customer,
- show your appreciation for customer referrals,
- send "we miss you" notes, and
- spotlight a loyal customer once a week/month.

Personalize your acts of appreciation to your customers.

"Hi [first name],

I just wanted to say thank you for being a [your company] customer! If there's anything I can do for you, reply to this email.

Have a great day!

[Email Signature]"

CELEBRATE THE WINS OF OTHERS

An engaged leader (formal and informal) gets team members talking about the wins and successes of other team members. Let's say you and another team member apply for the same promotional position, but your team member is selected for the role. This is where self-analysis, self-transformation, and self-evolution can shape the trajectory of a celebratory reaction. A typical reaction can vary between envy, resentment, feeling dejected, and asking yourself the question, "Why not me?" Oftentimes what is lacking in our society is happiness for one another. You, as a leader of yourself, can facilitate and contribute to celebratory recognition acts for your team member. Consider your options, such as giving your team member a congratulations card, a relevant book, or a gift card. Ask your team member how you can best support their transition into the new role. *MOVE* forward and continue to do what's necessary to learn, grow, and evolve in your career.

GOING BEYOND THE FOR-PROFIT BUSINESS WITH GRATITUDE

One organization I love to volunteer for is the Harris County Houston Sports Authority. The organization provides oversight to sports venues and promotes sporting events. In 2021, I served as a volunteer for an event hosted by Harris County, the 2021 AAU Junior Olympics. It was a great experience. Among the many competitions held (including wheelchair racing), I got to work the swim and pickleball competitions. I have to admit, I was exhausted after working the five days (five shifts—each consisting of six hours), but I was grateful for the opportunity to witness the upcoming generation of Olympic athletes and meet the volunteers from diverse cultures and backgrounds. Plus, it's always a bonus that the organization feeds us very well, and the volunteer leaders never miss an opportunity to tell you how grateful they are for your presence.

About a month later, I received a typed letter consisting of three long paragraphs from the CEO in the mail. She went on and on, talking about being grateful for the service and support of volunteers. Included with the letter was a pink index card, which included a handwritten note from one of the volunteer team members. I wanted to share the contents of the handwritten note:

> "Bridgette,
>
> Thank you for volunteering for the AAU Junior Olympics Games! We appreciate all your hard work throughout the week. Because of you, the event was a huge success!
>
> [Name of volunteer leader] and the HCHSA Volunteer Team"

While driving on your "Now what?" journey, it's important to include what matters most in your life. For me, it's not about money, the house I live in, the contents in my home, the car I drive, the clothes I wear, the restaurants where I eat, or the places I was blessed to travel. It will be the impressions I made and the lives I impacted.

Now that we've spent a significant amount of time slowing down to show our gratitude, think about a "Now what?" moment. Like writing someone a gratitude note right now. All you need is a pen and some paper. Maybe it's to a family member for hosting a family gathering. Maybe it's to someone who gave you advice about something. Maybe it's to someone who shared encouraging words during a time you were sad about a situation. Maybe it's to another parent who picked up your child from school. Maybe it's to a coworker who helped you with a project. Maybe it's the person who worked on your car at the repair shop. Maybe it's the person who maintains your lawn. Maybe it's to your neighbor for placing your trashcan near your garage.

Think about how you'll share the note, whether face-to-face, by US mail, via text message, through email, or a private message on social media. What will you say? Jot down some ideas below:

_____

_____

_____

_____

_____

I love this quote by Cynthia Ozick, who says, "We often take for granted the very things that most deserve our gratitude."

Rest Stop Exercise #7

A BE to Remember: Be Appreciative.

Appreciation communicated among coworkers will build strong collaborative relationships, affirm value to the team, and achieve team goals.

M   **O**   **V**   **E**

Master   **Omit**   **Visualize**   **Execute**

What do you need to master to show your gratitude in new and creative ways?

PERSONAL

_____

_____

_____

_____

_____

PROFESSIONAL

_____

_____

_____

_____

_____

What unwanted passengers do you need to omit?

PERSONAL

_____

_____

_____

_____

_____

_____

PROFESSIONAL

_____

_____

_____

_____

_____

_____

What actions do you visualize for showing gratitude?

PERSONAL

_____

_____

_____

_____

_____

_____

_____

PROFESSIONAL

_____

_____

_____

_____

_____

_____

_____

How will you execute your action plan?

PERSONAL

_____

_____

_____

_____

_____

_____

_____

PROFESSIONAL

_____

_____

_____

_____

_____

_____

_____

NOTES

Chapter 8

Staying in Park on the Golden Rule

*My humanity is bound up in yours, for
we can only be human together.*

—Desmond Tutu

In Chapter 3, I talked about the demonstrated actions of someone who is fed up. One example I gave was the driver who throws their middle finger up in the air toward another driver because the driver did not let their car pass. Has that ever happened to you? I know it's happened to me, and I couldn't think of a qualifying reason that would warrant such action. Maybe I was driving too slowly?

I'm sure you've heard and read about how aggressive driving incidents are on the rise across the country. In the county where I live, one of our news outlets reported a total of 246 road rage crashes in all of 2020 compared to 142 by the beginning of July 2021. They talked about aggressive behaviors such as excessive speeding, following too closely, multiple lane changes without signaling, unreasonable use of vehicle horns, obscene gestures, and other acts of aggression directed at motorists. It seems as though there's a new culture of people who haven't been taught the golden rule: Treat others the way you want to be treated.

Make no mistake about it. Your kids are watching you. Your neighbors are watching. People from various parts of your life are watching you. They are watching how and why you make your decisions. Even if they are a close ally, they are observing how you treat others. You can't simply blame someone else for your actions. You have to exercise the responsibility, address the root cause for unfavorable actions, and work your plan to MOVE.

ARE YOU LIVING YOUR LIFE PARKED ON THE GOLDEN RULE?

People will respond according to how they are treated. How do you want to be treated by others? Do you want to be treated with kindness? Do you want your family, your neighbors, your coworkers, or a stranger to help you when you're in need of assistance? How do you treat people like your family members, your neighbors, your coworkers, or strangers? Your actions toward others will undeniably determine their actions toward you. It's really that simple. Treat others the way you want to be treated. But when you put the pedal to the metal and travel the road you're on that needs to be repaired, replaced, or reconfigured, it just may not be that simple.

WHAT WILL THEY SAY?

A few years ago, I asked six people in my circle about myself to gauge my impact on others. This type of self-consciousness from external sources helped me to understand how others saw my treatment of them. The results helped me strengthen my relationships and focused my attention on having more positive interactions. Since that exercise, I know I've fallen short on more than one occasion. Just in case you want to gauge people in your inner circle, check out some sample questions to provoke your thoughts about questions you can ask them.

Family

1. How have I grown in my life through the years?
2. What have you seen as the most inspiring for me?
3. What negative behaviors or habits have consumed my life over the years?
4. What positive behaviors or habits have consumed my life over the years?
5. How have my friendships flourished over my life?
6. What friendships or relationships have stifled my growth?
7. When were you most concerned about me? What made you concerned?
8. When were you most impressed with me? What made you impressed?
9. Where do I still need to expand my understanding of myself?
10. How would you describe my personality?

Friends

1. What is something I do with intention to further my growth?
2. What is something meaningful that I bring to my relationships?
3. What relationships do I pursue that have a negative impact?
4. What mental and emotional struggles have you observed in me?
5. What have you seen as the most inspiring for me?
6. What brings me the most fulfillment in life?

7. What is my mindset when facing challenges?

8. What do I do that limits my pursuit of new experiences?

9. What would you list as my top five personal core values? Why?

10. What is my influence on others?

11. How would you describe my personality?

Significant Other

1. What are my most appealing characteristics?

2. How have you seen me evolve in our relationship?

3. What have you seen as the most inspiring for me?

4. What would you list as my top five personal core values? Why?

5. What areas of my life do you believe I struggle in?

6. How do I handle disappointments and setbacks?

7. How mindful am I of my feelings and influence on others?

8. What am I most intentional about in life?

9. How would you describe my personality?

I hope these questions will aid you in improving your consciousness. Consciousness from an external perceptive can be crucial to helping you foster better relationships and treating others the way you want to be treated. Don't be afraid to ask questions and listen to feedback.

The road so many people are traveling is dark. I know because I've been there. I have made countless decisions to exit the dark roads and take other roads that contribute to investing in myself—the detours that offered a path leading to a better disposition and outcome. All of those paths have made me more mindful of my treatment of others. I have to be honest that like exercising, my detours have been plentiful but worth the investment. If the changes you implement are no longer working, you've got to make some adjustments and mix it up. The main point is to carve out the time and invest in yourself. You have to take responsibility for where you are and where you want to be. Having an "under-construction" state of mind will help in becoming more conscious about how you think, feel, act, and treat others.

THE IMPACT OF YOUR PROFESSIONAL LIFE

You've heard it over and over again. Employees don't leave companies. They leave leaders. If you are a leader or someone who aspires to be a titled leader in an organization, you have to think differently about how to approach and make all of your team members feel valued and appreciated. Don't wait for the exit interview or review periods to share with your employee something they could be doing differently or better.

Below is an example of treating someone the way you'd want to be treated:

> Paul has been a solid team leader for five years. In the last two weeks, however, he has come in late four times. Yesterday, you received a complaint against Paul that he rudely told a customer to leave if he wasn't happy. When you (the division chief) met with Paul and asked him about what was going on, he told you he was having a tough time at home. Before the end of the day, you overheard Paul bluntly tell a customer that he would answer her question after she waited in line like everybody else. The customer walked out the door.

> Toward the end of the workday, you ask Paul to meet with you in the small meeting room. You say to Paul, "I observed you being short with one of our customers. She was so upset by what you said, she just left."

> Paul said, "Oh, I didn't realize. I'm sorry. My home issues are really weighing on me. My wife and I are having issues. We're contemplating getting a divorce."

> "Sounds like you're going through a difficult time, and I'm sorry to hear that. But right now, we're talking about the customer's experience. It's your job to politely acknowledge our customers, answer their questions, and treat them like guests."

> You further explain to Paul what role he plays in the big picture and what success looks like. You state, "Everyone has to do their part (for successful outcomes) to achieve the organization's objectives and mission.

> At the end of the conversation, you provide Paul with a pamphlet regarding the employer-sponsored employee assistance plan (EAP), and you documented your conversation with Paul.

> After observing Paul for a few days, you're happy about the improvements he's made in his delivery. You have the following conversation with Paul:

> "I saw you go above and beyond to follow up with the unhappy customer you had this morning to make sure she was completely satisfied. When you do that, you turn an unhappy customer into a loyal customer which is a win-win for everyone affiliated with the company. The five Rs—Relationships, Retention, Referrals, Reputation, and Revenue—we've discussed during our team meetings are achieved. Now tell me, how can I support you to ensure you provide that same service consistently to future customers?"

In the workplace, our relationships with others are paramount to our success in the organization. Today's employers are more focused than ever on team dynamics. They know most of the people applying to be a part of their organization will have the technical skills to do the job, but being engaged in, enthusiastic about, or committed (heart and soul) to the organization (the work environment) is not a given. Employers around the globe are realizing that a lack of employee engagement is impacting productivity, creativity, collaboration, service levels—their bottom-line. So, they are targeting a focus on "employee engagement—the employee experience" to help shape the culture of the organization, thereby creating a supportive infrastructure that nurtures growth and success.

THE GOLDEN RULE IN THE WORKPLACE

Be careful of workplace conversations that contain critical rather than complimentary comments. Would you like to be one of the people being spoken negatively about in the following examples?

- It's challenging to move forward because of Mr. T's limited knowledge of technology! Can you suggest he take a class? LOL!

- Now, exactly what does Sally do all day? Because it's not work!

- Mrs. J doesn't remember anything you tell her about our production updates. OMG! It's all good, though, because I can focus on something else. She's so frustrating!

- Sarah's so angry about her divorce and custody situation. That's why no one on the team wants to approach her to discuss project deliverables!

- Don't get caught in a conversation with Monty. He'll just want to talk about his golfing. He's so self-centered! All you can do is be quiet and just listen.

Options for careful handling:

- If the conversation about someone in the workplace is not positive, pivot away. Harmful workplace chit-chat will inhibit the team's productivity and make the non-participants feel uncomfortable.

- Redirect the conversation to one focused on training, brainstorming, and problem-solving rather than providing comment and/or confirmation.

- Direct the person to share their complaint, concern, and/or frustration face-to-face to their colleague, employee, or team member, not you.

- Stop them before they get started. Don't normalize critical/unfavorable conversations and feedback about others in the workplace.

CONSEQUENCES WHEN THE GOLDEN RULE IN THE WORKPLACE IS MISSING

- Trust will be slaughtered.
- Feelings will be hurt.
- Morale will be damaged.
- Reputations will be tarnished.
- Personal and professional credibility will be tainted.
- Apprehension will be birthed.
- Dissension will be felt.

Whether you're a titled leader in your organization or someone others look up to, you impact the golden rule in the workplace. So, leaders (formal and informal), how are you training/influencing the people in your workplace on how to (1) have an open, honest relationship, (2) give direct feedback, and (3) have difficult conversations with their colleagues, employees, and team members?

As the golden rule states, treat your colleagues, your employees, and your team members the way you would want to be treated every day. No guessing is needed. Next-level results will happen in the workplace.

BENEFITS OF THE GOLDEN RULE IN THE WORKPLACE

When you're truthful, transparent, respectful, fair, supportive, flexible, informative, and committed to your colleagues, employees, and team members, next-level success will happen in the workplace.

Benefits:

- Effective communication
- A focus on goals and results
- Targeted planning
- Continuous collaboration

THE GOLDEN RULE IS A CHEMISTRY BUILDER

Imagine you're the leader of a team, and your team is not doing as well as expected. Your boss has instructed you to better challenge your team members or contact human resources to start the "get rid of" process. That is, get rid of the employees who are not performing. Well, in your case, that would be the whole team.

Now consider yourself as not the leader, but as one of the team members your boss wants you to "get rid of." How would you want to be treated? I know I would want the leader to sit down with me to have a conversation about my job performance and not meeting expectations. You can learn a lot through listening and discussing. You may find out the employee does not trust you. The employee may not feel challenged. The employee may feel you do not believe in them or do not want to see them succeed and grow. It's important for you to better understand any possible contributing reasons to team members' poor performance.

As a leader, you must recognize that there are three reasons for poor performance:

A Lack of Communication: They Don't Know What's Expected of Them

- There is a lack of clear, individualized communication and direction.
- There is a lack of feedback.
- There are mixed messages from different leaders.

A Lack of Conditions: They Need More Help to Succeed

- They need more time.
- They need more resources.
- They need more training.

A Lack of Consequences: They See That Nothing Happens One Way or the Other

- They see no encouragement on previous good work.
- They see no recognition for good work.
- They see no repercussions for poor work.

Before you can be sure your challenge is fair, you have to determine whether the team member has been given a fair chance to perform well. Take another minute to ask yourself three questions.

- Have I clearly communicated what I expect?
- Are there conditions that hinder them?
- Are there clear consequences for their performance?

COMMUNICATION: DID I CLEARLY COMMUNICATE WHAT I EXPECTED OUT OF THEIR PERFORMANCE?

One way to understand that you have communicated clearly is to encourage your team members to ask questions. "Is there anything about this that isn't quite clear?" Let them know you expect questions to arise, and you are available at any time to answer them. You could say, "I know that once we get into this, there are probably going to be a lot more questions, so please stop me whenever you have one." Remember, inviting a lot of questions on the front end of a new project or procedural change can save you hours of cleanup headaches later on in the process.

WHAT WILL THEY SAY?

As we did in the exercise before, it's time to gauge the people in your inner circle. Check out some sample questions to provoke your thoughts about questions you can ask the following people that make up your workplace inner circle.

Team Member:

1. What are my top five qualities in the workplace? Why?
2. What contributions do I make to the work environment?
3. Am I a supportive team member?
4. How have I contributed to the growth of our team?
5. What improvements can I make to contribute to growth in the company?
6. What would you list as my top five personal core values? Why?
7. How well do I communicate with others? Where can I improve?

Boss:

1. What are my top five qualities in the workplace? Why?
2. What are three things I can do better immediately?
3. How do my team members, customers, clients, etc. describe me?
4. How have I contributed to the growth of our team?
5. What improvements can I make to grow in the company?
6. What would you list as my top five personal core values? Why?
7. Would you view me as dependable, trustworthy, and flexible?
8. How well do I communicate with others? Where can I improve?

Employees:

1. How well do I support you, your work, and your career aspirations?
2. How well do I communicate goals, objectives, initiatives, and expectations with you and the team? Where can I improve?
3. Have I created an environment that allows you to be creative?

4. What are five things I can do immediately to better support my employees?

5. What would you list as my top five personal core values? Why?

As previously stated, an external perspective can be crucial to helping you foster better relationships and treating others the way you want to be treated in the workplace.

Rest Stop Exercise #8

A BE to Remember: Be a Connector.

The best principle of life we can all live by is to treat others the way we want to be treated.

M O V E

Master **Omit** **Visualize** **Execute**

What do you need to master to be thoughtful and empathetic toward others?

PERSONAL

_____

_____

_____

_____

_____

_____

PROFESSIONAL

_____

_____

_____

_____

_____

_____

What unwanted passengers do you need to omit?

PERSONAL

_____

_____

_____

_____

_____

_____

PROFESSIONAL

_____

_____

_____

_____

_____

_____

What action activities do you visualize?

PERSONAL

_____

_____

_____

_____

_____

_____

PROFESSIONAL

_____

_____

_____

_____

_____

_____

How will you execute your action plan?

PERSONAL

_____

_____

_____

_____

_____

_____

PROFESSIONAL

_____

_____

_____

_____

_____

_____

NOTES

Chapter 9

Allowing Authorized Personnel Only on Your Road to Freedom

Too many of us are not living our dreams because we are living our fears.

—Les Brown

The road of life can be freeing and filled with opportunities to be creative while incorporating new experiences. It can be fun, adventurous, and scary. In 2017, Tracy, my best running friend I talked about earlier, invited me to be on a team she was on for a Ragnar Relay because someone had dropped out. A Ragnar Relay is a team of twelve individuals who will run approximately two hundred miles—from point A to point B—on city streets, country roads, sidewalks, and bike paths. The individuals run a relay format day, and night, and day again, sleeping in vans and grassy fields taking anywhere from twenty-four to thirty-six hours to complete. I was somewhat hesitant when I read the description of the race.

Tracy has a way of convincing me to do interesting and fun stuff. She introduced me to Roderick, the team captain, and I agreed to run in the event. The team received weeks of instructions and protocols. Safety was paramount. You were told to be prepared to run at night and in varied weather conditions (rain, lightning, thunderstorms, and extreme heat).

My team of twelve was called Team Pace Cadets. When the time arrived for the event, we all met in Austin, Texas, to start our journey together. We were separated into two groups of six and rode in two Suburban vans. We started our race on a Friday morning in Bastrop, Texas, and ended on the following Saturday afternoon in Luckenbach, Texas. We relay raced two hundred miles, handing off a baton between twelve individuals for over eighteen hours straight. We ran, chatted, and slept in a van during our time together. I had three legs of the race totaling 19.7 miles, one which required me to run at night.

I was a solo runner at night on a country road in some small town. I had purchased special products for the race, but what I remember vividly is the bath wipes. When you're in a van with people who are eating, using the restroom, and running day and night, those wipes are an essential item. I had purchased a headlamp and reflective vest for my night running. The Ragnar Race was a fun and unforgettable experience. We got a medal and a shirt before heading back home as Ragnarians.

You received the abbreviated version of my Ragnar Relay adventure, but I could write another book talking about the twenty-four-plus hours of endless conversations with my team members (who, other than Tracy, were strangers), waiting for team members to finish their race leg, eating and sleeping with six people in a van, the scenic road sites, the charm of restaurants in the small towns we visited, and the agony of running my legs in the highest heat of the day, on rolling hills, and at night.

One of my horrifying moments was running upon a corpse of an animal. I can't remember if it was a dog or a deer. I avoided looking at it as I ran past and as far to my right on the two-lane road as I could. I just remember the horrible smell.

The Ragnar Relay has by far been one of my greatest running adventures, mainly because it was a team effort that required us to extend ourselves beyond the usual grit and determination. We ran, drove, slept, and repeated to achieve.

The roads of life can be exciting and adventurous as well as agonizing and scary, but you can't let something agonizing and scary stifle your pursuits. Free yourself and be ready to experience something new that challenges you. My stance in life is to be emboldened to move in such a way I'm always in discovery mode, I'm always ready to tackle the next thing on my journey, and I'm always excited about making new memories.

EVOLUTION REQUIRES YOU TO BE CLEAR, CALM, AND COMMITTED

Self-evolution requires you to invest in you—your time, your effort, and your money. All of that constitutes your treasure. When the time comes to achieve something new and/or different in your life—a job, a promotion, a business, a new house, a stress-free life, a disease-free life, a healthier lifestyle, an adventure—it's important that the person outline their strategy for achieving that thing. How are you going to strategize your time, effort, and money to achieve? Your strategy—inclusive of a clear, calm, and committed mindset—will make your road to freedom and creativity much easier.

A great example of people who strategize freedom and creativity to the fullest are competitive athletes playing for a championship title. Let's think about the sport of basketball as an example. Four teams compete to play in the championship finals, hustling and sacrificing their bodies. To win, they understand the importance of a clear, calm, and committed mindset. They are clear about what they need to do, calm as they contribute their skills and talents, and committed to the success of the team—three important ingredients for evolution.

BE A LIFELONG LEARNER

Evolution happens with a passion for learning. Learning leads to freedom and creativity. There's so much to consider when we talk about learning, such as the uniqueness of other cultures, what makes the different generations in the workplace tick, the fine details regarding the formation of the organization where you work, and the leadership team with its vision, mission, and values.

Be committed to increasing your exposure to people and things. Always be in learning mode. Make the necessary investments—time, energy, and money—to continuously improve and grow personally and professionally throughout your life.

You have the power to authorize the things you can focus on to improve personally, such as:

- joining a fitness group;
- trying a new fitness activity;
- taking a cooking class to explore and incorporate healthier eating options. Researching activities that facilitate getting adequate sleep; and
- traveling to new destinations.

Note: Increasing your exposure and learning can contribute to finding commonalities, building rapport, and maintaining relationships that create strong bonds to foster constructive conversations and impactful collaboration, thereby contributing to your personal growth. You may not have everything figured out, but your "under-construction" PPP can serve as your blueprint. You'll add new and different activities as you expand your thoughts. Exposure leads to expanded thoughts, different cultures, different age groups, different races, and different nationalities.

THE IMPACT ON YOUR PROFESSIONAL LIFE

As you consider ways to improve your life, self-evolution—as it pertains to your road to freedom and creativity—must include an expansion in your perspective about your professional growth. Always be thinking of ways you can stand out among team members, peers, and company leaders. Authorizing yourself to engage in the following activities can be paramount to your expansion:

Don't be afraid to mix and mingle. During a company meeting that included subordinates, peers, department leaders, and the CEO comparable in the agency, I remembered hearing that the CEO comparable had lost a significant amount of weight because of a lifestyle change. Prior to the start of the meeting, I noticed the CEO comparable standing off to the side alone. I decided to go over and inquire about his lifestyle change. We engaged in a brief dialogue about the steps he had taken to facilitate his weight loss journey. When I returned back to the area where my group was standing, you'd think I'd had a face-to-face conversation with God. Upon my return, I was greeted with, "You went over there and talked to Mr. Man. I can't believe you did that." The point is—don't be afraid to talk to the leaders in your organization. You may end up being the first one in the room with them or caught in the elevator with them. Make the most of the opportunity. Inquire about their day, say something about a company accomplishment, or be like me and mention a known topic about him or her, such as their completion of a marathon. It's also a good reason to always know the happenings in your organization. You just never know—your interactions with higher-ups may contribute to an advancement opportunity.

Don't be afraid to speak up. How many times have you been in the meeting and wanted to ask a question about something being discussed? You didn't ask because of higher-ups in the room. Or because you were afraid your voice might quiver. Or because you didn't believe your question would come across as pertinent. People who are intentional about getting noticed by those who impact career progression don't wait for permission or an invitation to speak. Maybe it's because I like to talk to people, but I never miss an opportunity to ask a question, inquire further about something being vetted, or contribute my thoughts about a change. If you've familiarized yourself with the topic of discussion and anticipate how the discussion may evolve beyond the topic prior to the meeting, then you'll be prepared to ask a well-thought-out question or offer a suggestion, thereby contributing to the discussion. You just never know—your contributions to conversations involving higher-ups may contribute to an advancement opportunity.

Don't shy away from taking the lead. I'm sure you've been involved in a workplace situation that needs someone to step up. Let's consider a scenario where the manager is sick and out of office, and something has gone terribly wrong with the widgets production line. You don't want to be one of the team members who say, "There's nothing we can do until Mike returns from being sick. Hopefully, the line will not be down more than a day or so." No, this is your opportunity to think and act like a manager. Always know someone is watching and will report back to the higher-ups. This is your opportunity to think strategically about what needs to be done to get the widgets production line back up and running properly and move to get it done. You just never know—your move to take the lead and get the production line back on track may contribute to an advancement opportunity.

Don't be afraid to get involved or do more. In so many companies, there are opportunities to join committees or participate in activities beyond the scope of your job description. During the time I worked for a school district, an annual superintendent's fun run was created. I was fairly new to the agency at the time it was created. Because my boss at the time knew I was an avid runner, she thought I'd be a good fit to join the fun run committee. She went a step further and inquired about getting me on the committee. Your company could be instituting a new safety initiative, a fundraiser for a charitable organization, or revamping its technology infrastructure and need representatives from the different departments to help with initiation, planning, and execution. Getting involved in other aspects of your company is a great way to meet other company employees and learn more about your company and opportunities of greater interest to you. You just never know—your involvement in other aspects of the company may contribute to an advancement opportunity.

Don't be afraid to share your ideas. I'm sure you've noticed processes in your organization that can be streamlined, done better, or more effectively. The mark of a committed and caring employee is one who shares how simple modifications and fixes can improve the department's operations. It's funny, but when people share their frustrations with me about things that could be performed differently and better in their work environment, I typically get the same responses: "I tried to tell them, but they don't want to make any changes. They like things as is. They don't want to make any improvements." So, I follow up by asking, "Did you clearly share your ideas and recommendations (to include benefits, impact on the business, and implementation strategy) in writing?" A repeated response is, "They won't read it." You just never know—going above and beyond to write and submit your ideas and recommendations may be a contributing factor to an advancement opportunity.

Don't forget to be inclusive. Let's consider an example where you've achieved your goal of becoming a business owner or a manager/supervisor in your organization. At some point in your respective leadership role, someone will ask you the question, "What are you doing to switch the dial on creating progressive inclusion?"

You're probably asking yourself, *What does this have to do with being fed up?* If you're operating in a "fed-up" state, you won't be able to expand your perspective. You won't be able to operate with clarity on charting your plan to be a better you, employee, team member, manager, or supervisor. Regarding your professional life, you want to understand and recognize the benefits of an expanded perspective, respecting and accepting others for their differences, or including others regardless of their personal perspectives, preferences, and personalities. When you dive in with a focus on learning about and understanding others, you discover commonalities and realize you're not so different after all. Benefits pertaining to your company or personal business include things like enhanced people interactions, expanded growth, increased profits, better service levels, better decisions, and increased innovation.

Professional development may mean:

A skilled employee is a valued asset. The more you can sharpen your skills (digital, analytical, soft, and leadership), the more beneficial it is for the company. Be willing to set aside time and/or money for:

- attending webinars, seminars, and conferences;
- reading books, white papers, and trade journals;
- listening to radio stations with differing viewpoints;
- listening to podcasts;
- studying a new subject;
- joining networking organizations;
- learning a different language or how to use a new technology platform; and
- completing a professional certification program.

Do you think your company connections make you a shoo-in candidate for that next-level position? Just because you already work for the company or have connections to higher-ups and decision-makers does not mean you will be the selected candidate when the time for upward movement arrives. It's likely you'll be competing with internal and external candidates, so it is critical to make sure you put your best foot forward through targeted preparation and planning.

Do not take the online application process for granted. All hiring representatives want to see each section of the online application thoroughly completed. Never write, "See Resume." Most recruiters and hiring managers will translate that statement to "incomplete application." They will scroll on to the next applicant.

If you do not know the addresses, telephone numbers, etc. of companies you have worked for in the past, now is the time to look up (Google) the information. Even if your resume provides a summary of the job responsibilities, the same information must be included on your online application.

Make the summary of your job responsibilities consist of complete descriptive sentences. Employers are verifying work history information, so make sure you have dates of employment and salary information indicated on your online application. The "reason for leaving" section can be a tricky area to complete if you were terminated, resigned in lieu of termination, or resigned without providing the employer a two-week notice. You may consider writing, "Will discuss during interview."

Whether your intentions are to promote within your current organization or explore opportunities in other organizations, think and plan. Create your ninety-day entry plan. Preparation means you will already know or seek to gain a deeper understanding of the current or potential organization's operations, values, culture, history, and workforce. To a current or potential employer, the ninety-day entry plan reflects your priorities and strong desire to make a thoughtful and deliberate assessment of and entry into the organization. It demonstrates your strategy for gathering information from stakeholders to ensure (1) achievements of short-term and long-term goals and expected outcomes, (2) strategies to identify and address concerns and solve problems, and (3) assessments related to relevant policies and standard operating procedures support and enhance the operations of the organization.

In a discussion with a client, Thelma, about her role as a team leader in the seafood department for a national grocery chain, she wanted advice about increasing her chances to promote to a higher-level managerial position. She talked about the growth of the company and how she wanted to become the lead in the seafood department that would soon be available at a new store. Based on the information she shared with me, I knew she was an effective team leader. Her ability to handle additional responsibilities, train her team members, motivate and lead her team on the completion of successful projects, manage the day-to-day operations, and create performance reports. She didn't sound like someone who missed deadlines, failed to be timely when responding to emails/requests for information, nor someone who gossiped about other employees. She didn't just talk about her job responsibilities, she talked about her contributions to improving their department—updating standard operating procedures related to the safety and sanitary handling and processing of fish and working with the fish chefs to create a selection of store-prepared, take-home fish dishes. I could tell Thelma was someone committed to learning about her company, keeping up with changes in her industry of work, and she was in the loop about changes/expansions happening within her company.

I explained to Thelma what it takes to lead a department and that she needed to outline her strategy. I explained to her that her pursuit of becoming a department leader required her to think bigger than a team leader because she would be managing the various aspects of seafood products, interacting with vendors, and solving problems on a higher level in the grocery store chain.

Below is an excerpt of my conversation with Thelma:

Me: What is the vision for your company?

Thelma: To sustain its position as the world's leader in natural and organic foods.

Me: What role does the seafood department play in that vision?

Thelma: To provide the highest standard of wild-caught and farm-raised seafood.

Me: You know what is coming down the pipeline. Don't delay your preparation. You will need to show management you have mastered the leadership skills necessary for leading the seafood department. That you have a strategy—that you have outlined your long-term goals and broken them into executable tasks and performance indicators related to responsibilities like achieving sales, purchasing, and labor targets, growing and developing your team, modeling and delivering outstanding customer service, and managing the safe handling of products.

All of the things we discussed, I wanted her to treat them as a setup for a future return on her investments (ROI). If she continued to do what was necessary to move to the next level, then there was a high probability of gaining a return on her investments. Your ROI may result in improved communication skills, higher level of confidence, better planning skills, expanded productivity, superior quality of work, and increased job satisfaction.

We all work to be good at the skills listed in our job descriptions, but the most successful people are always thinking, *Now what do I need to know and achieve to obtain and be successful in my next role*? Think about knowledge you should be obtaining and skills you should be developing and/or enhancing. Write down what comes to your mind:

_____

_____

_____

_____

_____

I asked Liletta, Daniel, and Tony about their perspective on success and failure, which can greatly affect professional development. They all had enlightening responses.

- **Liletta:** I don't view any of the things that didn't work as failures. I view them as lessons. When I'm passionate about something, I go for it. Sometimes it doesn't work how I planned. Sometimes, the people that relate to that particular venture don't come through for me, but it's all okay because there is always a lesson. That lesson will help me make the next venture successful. My advice is to scale down what you need to feel successful in your business. Strip away the monetary gains and focus on how you will feel—that sense of satisfaction in knowing you are walking in your purpose. Work toward that, and you can't fail.

- **Daniel:** I had to learn that you will have failures when starting a business. If you put together a good business and believe in what you are doing, you will eventually have success. I walked away from my online fragrance business once my vendor started to change products. I believe if I would have stayed with that business, I would have made it a success. As a real estate agent, I could have quit the first year I did not sell a house. My people walked from real estate at first because they were looking to make money fast. I stayed with real estate and have sold over fifty homes as a part-time realtor. To me, success as a realtor is not only making money but seeing people get the home of their dreams.

- **Tony:** I don't believe I've ever failed. Failure is having an experience where I didn't learn anything. I always try to learn from every experience, both good and bad.

Rest Stop Exercise #9

A BE to Remember: Be Knowledgeable.

Whether it pertains to the personal or professional life, you want to always pursue opportunities to learn. The end result is your freedom to choose to BE.

M   O   V   E

Master   Omit   Visualize   Execute

What in your "right now" do you need to master to increase
your knowledge and facilitate your learning?

PERSONAL

_____

_____

_____

_____

_____

_____

PROFESSIONAL

_____

_____

_____

_____

_____

_____

_____

What unwanted passengers do you need to omit?

PERSONAL

_____

_____

_____

_____

_____

_____

PROFESSIONAL

_____

_____

_____

_____

_____

_____

What action activities should you visualize?

PERSONAL

_____

_____

_____

_____

_____

_____

PROFESSIONAL

_____

_____

_____

_____

_____

_____

How will you execute your action plan?

PERSONAL

_____

_____

_____

_____

_____

_____

PROFESSIONAL

_____

_____

_____

_____

_____

_____

NOTES

SELF-NARRATION

Chapter 10

Entering Your Low Overhead Clearance of Truth

The road to success is always under construction. It is a progressive course, not an end to be reached.

—Tony Robbins

Before the days of GPS (Global Positioning System), I remember the stories my girlfriends would share about road trips with their spouses. They talked about how their spouses would drive around and end up on roads that did not lead to their final destination. They spoke of the reluctance of their spouses to stop and ask for directions. One of my girlfriends shared, "I was reading the directions from my map to him. So many times, I'd tell him to either turn right, then left, go straight, or make a U-turn." She stated he'd respond, "I know where I'm going. We'll be there in thirty minutes." The one thing they'd never get from their spouses was the truth that they were lost. Of course, my girlfriends would be beyond fed up with a two-hour drive that would turn into five hours.

When you think about the top areas of one's life that matter most—family, friends, finances, health/fitness, career/business, community, and leisure/fun—what truths are you holding back? Are you driving around lost? Are you driving around unhappy and unfulfilled? Are any of the areas contributing to a "fed-up" state? Should any areas be under construction? No one is stuck with the life they have. You can always create and activate a plan to progressively move forward, but always remember that a plan is only as good as the action behind it.

I know I don't have to tell you. You can achieve your personal and professional goals at any age. You can be happy and have fun at any age. You can exert your ability to analyze, plan, and respond with intention at any age, which will give you the ability to reach your destination with less of a chance of getting lost along the way. All you need is to be locked in and loaded with confidence. But your mobility is restricted as you're trying to navigate your life in a "fed-up" state.

FAMILY/FRIENDS

Are your relationships with your spouse, parents, child, sibling, or other family members the way you would want them to be? Are your relationships with your friends the way you would want them to be? I've discovered that when you're fed up in some aspect of your life, your family and friend relationships may not be all they can be. Who knows? It may be because of a family or friend situation that you're fed up. I won't go in depth on discussions about family and friends in this section, as I've talked a lot about people and relationships in the preceding chapters. I think you get the points I wanted to make. The one extra point I'd like to make is to make sure you borrow the positive stuff from your family and friends. Stuff like faith, hope, strength, courage, integrity, confidence, compassion, and drive to move forward with achieving your "Now what?"

FINANCES

Are you fed up with the state of your finances? Maybe it's because you're living paycheck to paycheck. Maybe it's because you have five credit cards with a $5,000 limit, and you're at the limit on all five. Maybe it's because you're about to lose your car for failure to pay your payday loan. Perhaps you had a single-person car accident, and the costs of repairs are lower than the deductible, but you don't have the money to get your car repaired. You might be stressed.

CONSEQUENCES OF FINANCIAL TROUBLES

Financial challenges can lead to homelessness, sleeping in your car, or staying with a friend or relative who has given you an exit date. You're trying to get a home or apartment, but your credit score is preventing you from such or making your options very expensive. You allowed the insurance on your car to lapse, and now you can't get car insurance from a reputable company because of your credit. You've gotten citations for no car insurance and your expired registration. You didn't pay either one, so there's a warrant out for your arrest. You can't get utilities in your name because of your credit. You can't find a friend or family member to cosign for you. You no longer have the car you were sleeping in because the repossession company picked it up at your job. Now you don't have reliable transportation to work. One more tardy at work, and you'll be terminated.

THE ROOT CAUSE

Whether you make $75,000 annually or $150,000 annually, you can find yourself fed up because the state of your finances is out of control. If any of the descriptions above fits your "right now," there is some good news. When it comes to finances, you have to identify, study, and analyze the root cause. Are your financial troubles a result of not being financially prepared for that unexpected medical bill, car repair, citation, or helping a relative with a financial matter, or do your financial troubles stem from buying things to impress or compete with others? Are you buying things to prove you belong, to show you measure up, or to be accepted? These can all be a never-ending cycle that lands you owing more than you can pay. You might have qualified for and purchased more house than you could afford. Perhaps you purchased a luxury car that costs an arm and a leg to maintain, participated in excessive spending, and only make $75,000 annually. You might brag about paying $200, $300, $400, or more for a pair of shoes, or you might boast about going to the spa once a month for self-care. If you make $150,000 annually, you may brag about your cruises and travels to exotic places or boast about eating at upscale restaurants.

Your scenario could be completely different. You might have been living within your salary guidelines, had money saved in your bank, and were on track to help your kids with college expenses. You might have paid off your home and car before the expected unexpected happened. Your spouse asked for a divorce, then the division of assets, property, debt, retirement funds, and taxes left you financially drained. Now you have to pay child support.

Your scenario could be a surgery that resulted in your out-of-pocket cost being $20,000. It could be the resolution of a family matter that resulted in a $30,000 legal bill, the $25,000 a friend convinced you to invest in a business that closed after six months, or the $2,000 a month you're contributing for the care of your parent living in a facility. This depletion of funds could have you financially devastated.

GETTING CAUGHT WITH APPEARANCES

No one knows someone's true financial state. All you really know is what someone shows and tells. Many years ago, I had a friend who was overwhelmed by a significant amount of financial debt. He had made some poor financial decisions living beyond his salary level, loaning money to family and friends, and making some risky financial investments. During this time, he was late on paying his bills or simply did not pay them at all. Because he had a good-paying job, he could still acquire things, but only at a higher cost.

Value lesson: INTEGRITY. Simply not paying debts at all after knowing and doing what is right is a contradiction of one's integrity.

WHAT IS YOUR CHILD'S TAKEAWAY?

If you're a parent or someone in a parental role, it's important to consider that your child(ren) is watching you and how you handle your money.

- Does your child see you pulling out the credit card for virtually every expenditure?

- Does your child hear you talk about ways to better manage your money, save money, have a household budget, and perform old-fashioned, do-it-yourself tasks?

- Do they see you trying to keep up with the way those in your inner circle are living?

- Are they accustomed to you routinely saying "yes" to your wants and their wants?

Kids will take on their parents' habits and values, so how well are you preparing your kids to live life without you—on their own—and be financially responsible and independent?

- Are you teaching your kid about having a savings account?

- Are you teaching your kid to pay cash and not charge?

- Are you teaching your kid not to buy everything they want? If not, there could be consequences.

- Will your adult kid still be living at home with you at the age of thirty-five or forty-five like he/she is a teenager, driving a fancy car, hanging out with friends at every opportunity, and buying the latest technology—cellular telephone or gadget?

- Will your adult kid be the one who returns home after college not eager about finding a job, spending his time at home during the day and operating your electricity at full blast while you're at work?

MASTER YOUR SPENDING MOMENTS

When it comes to money, we typically explore ways and options to make more money—a promotion, a higher paying job, an investment, a second job, or a side hustle—all of which is good. Questions to think about are how much you want to earn, how much you want to save, and what you need to do to eliminate your debt. An expanded perspective to have is learning how to maximize the money you make—to manage the pay you bring home and more effectively manage your financial life and prepare for your future. That's what you want to teach your kid.

MY TURN-AROUND PLAN

In Chapter 5, I talked about my exit plan from my last employer. When I determined that I needed to plan my exit, my finances were a huge concern. I was in debt, and I knew I couldn't continue to simply live day to day without outlining a clear path for the things I wanted to achieve.

I had to develop my strategic plan to live debt-free. First, I had to face my truth about how I got into debt, why debt was keeping me from living life the way I wanted to, and how I had become enslaved to my creditors. I devised a twenty-four-month strategic plan primarily focused on eliminating my financial debt, and the first order of financial business I tackled was my credit card debt. I created a spreadsheet listing all of my creditors, the amount owed to each one, and a payment/payoff timeline.

In 2019, I made the toughest of decisions. I committed to a year of only spending on my essential needs like my mortgage loan, car loan, utilities, and food. For me, it was a tough decision to give up retail spending. I set aside a certain amount of money for family and friends' birthdays, donations to organizations, and my running shoes, but there was absolutely no ancillary spending. Next on the list was to pay off my car loan, and I did. I accomplished the financial goals I had outlined for myself. By June 2020, I had positioned myself to exit the traditional workforce debt-free and open my HR consulting business, which I did.

Early in the book, I asked what you were passionate about. In my most recent "fed-up" state, I had worked in an unfulfilling position with no opportunity to make a difference. The only thing I was passionate about was helping others to be better. I could either stay in a position that paid me a lot of money to continue doing that, or I could pursue a passion that would bring me joy.

I decided to create and activate my "under-construction" PPP. I have found myself surrounded by people daily who are in some aspect of an unhappy or unfulfilled life, simply wanting to pursue their passions, dreams, and aspirations. Life's distractions and assaults sometimes don't allow a person to see a clear pathway to achieving their wants. I know it sounds cliché, but change really does start with you.

YOUR TURN-AROUND PLAN

You can turn your financial woes around. One of the values my parents instilled in me was to always maintain good credit. No matter how much debt I may have accrued, they planted the seed to always pay my bills and pay them on time, so paying bills was never an issue for me.

One of the things I did periodically was check my credit score. I wanted to make sure my credit score was always in a good range, and I'd advise you to do the same. I got free annual reports from Equifax, TransUnion, and Experian, which offered a variety of tools and resources to help you with understanding, repairing, and monitoring your credit. Just know if your credit is poor, you'll definitely get the worst deals. The main point is to always strive to maintain a high credit score. If you have a higher credit score, it just may be the key to receiving favorable credit terms, resulting in possible lower payments and interest for a house you've envisioned purchasing.

Some people have financial advisors/planners to help them with their finances and planning for the future, but I didn't need someone to tell me to stop spending and be intentional about living debt-free and financially independent. Check out the sample budget worksheet in the Your Under-Construction Worksheets section to jumpstart your analyzing process. It's a tool I used when I decided to face my financial reality. Doing so will help you face your truth about your "right now" financial situation and help you with your turn-around plan. Today, there are a lot of online apps, and you can download an Excel financial worksheet. With many of the tools, all you need to do is plug in your numbers. Once you've analyzed and outlined your take-home pay along with your monthly expenditures, you'll be in a better position to ask yourself:

- ✓ How can I redistribute my income?
- ✓ What expenses can I reduce or omit?
- ✓ What monies can I redirect to start paying off my credit card bills?
- ✓ How much can I start setting aside right now to jumpstart a savings account?

BE A METHODICAL MONEY MANAGER

One of the breeding grounds for workplace woes is an employee's financial health in distress because they believe they have to stay and endure. You shouldn't have to stay in a situation where you are unhappy and unfulfilled. Here's where self-truth sets in.

Is your desire to make a change stifled by money concerns? If so, your "under-construction" PPP will help you to formulate your ideas about money management. It will help you strategize the steps you can take to improve or remedy areas of spending. Change in your methodical money management can be simple things like:

- investing in lawn equipment and cutting your own yard,
- buying supplies to clean your own house,
- buying the ingredients to cook your own meals,
- buying a washing machine/dryer and cleaning supplies to wash/clean your own clothes,

- buying your own nail supplies to do a manicure and paint your own nails,
- driving to the store and doing your own grocery shopping,
- driving to the restaurant and picking up your own food,
- buying a coffee maker and your favorite coffee and making your own coffee at home,
- buying a blender and ingredients and making your own smoothie, and
- researching to get ideas from planning and decorating platforms and planning your own party/event.

No thinking outside the box is needed. It's just a matter of taking do-it-yourself to another level. Who knows? Your money management initiatives may lead to a happy and fulfilled life from a different perspective, such as your ability to fund your fun and leisure activities, which I'll discuss later in this chapter. If you're co-managing your money with a spouse or significant other, your under-construction process regarding managing money may end up under scrutiny, especially if your partner has a different perspective about spending, saving, giving, and investing.

HEALTH/FITNESS

Are you fed up with the state of your health and fitness? Do you feel as though you have no energy and are tired of dealing with the challenges and limitations of pain in your back, knee, shoulder, hip, or arm? If so, you might consider implementing some sort of exercise plan, but what if you don't see it as an option for you?

I remember many years ago when a customer commented on the running shirt I wore while standing in the grocery line. The customer said, "I wish I could run. I have bad knees and ACL tears in both knees. I wish I could be physically active. Maybe then I could get rid of this extra forty pounds I'm carrying and get off my high blood pressure and high cholesterol medication." Whether your situation is due to an injury or inflammation in your body, don't delay engaging in a discussion with your primary care physician to explore your options for being physically active. Depending on your particular situation, your primary care physician might recommend a pain manage- ment specialist, physical therapist, or personal trainer to help you. Research continues to show people of all ages and physical conditions benefit from exercise.

I have been a member of LA Fitness for well over ten years. Now that I have some extra time, I attend their daytime fitness classes. The beauty of attending during the day is that I get to interact with older women of varied ethnicities. After finishing in a mat Pilates class one day, I asked a lady how she liked the class. She shared that she was unable to do some of the poses because she had had a hip replacement and needed a second one. She talked about being in some pain, but she wasn't going to let it stop her from attending the class. I had such admiration for the lady and what she had shared about not letting it stop her.

I've had clients who faced discouraging thoughts about not being able to walk up a flight of stairs without becoming winded, physically engaging with their kids or grandkids five minutes without becoming exhausted, doing yard work like bending over to plant flowers or rake leaves without experiencing some level of pain, or standing for an extended period of time without pain. If you're having thoughts comparable to those of my clients, a pain management specialist, physical therapist, or personal trainer might be able to help you explore and recommend beneficial tools and exercises when overcoming/managing an injury or trying to manage/eliminate chronic pain. These can be stretching, balancing, or strength and flexibility exercises.

For the folks who do not have things like chronic pain as a consideration, getting started with some form of exercise can be hard. As a personal trainer and fitness coach, I've heard all of the reasons for inactivity like no time, family obligations, not enjoying exercising, being too busy, having hurt their feet in the military, not having childcare, or being their parent's care provider.

On your road to evolution in your health and fitness, I want you to install a sign that says, "No excuses allowed."

THE ROOT CAUSE AND CONSEQUENCES

In Chapter 5, I described my bout of inflammation raging throughout my body. For a period of time, I was under the care of a rheumatologist. When I hear someone talk about ailments like joint pain, bad back, and bad knees, I think about inflammation in the body and possible root causes like one's diet, stress, obesity, injury, diseases, and the environment.

When I think about the road to freedom and creativity, it's hard for someone to focus on anything if they suffer from constant aches and pain. You can't walk your dog, go up a flight of stairs, or walk from your car to the grocery store without pain. Until you discover the root cause and work with a medical professional to explore relief options, your road to freedom and creativity will remain stagnant. After you take control of your pain, you will be able to analyze and act to pursue your "Now what?" and live healthier.

As a human resources professional, I've met countless people in the workplace through the years who have come to work in pain most days, suffering from hurting knees, swollen hands, and back pain. I can think of two who would have been more creative, collaborative, and productive had it not been for their pain. While under the care of my rheumatologist, I was in the midst of running marathon events, doing personal training, and coaching beginner runners. Suddenly, limitations were placed on my life due to inflammation that came out of nowhere. Because of pain throughout my days, I forcibly focused on getting the job done in the midst of it, but I'm grateful to have been in remission for over fifteen years due to my rheumatologist's treatment plan.

I spoke to a group of coworkers about how unhealthy lifestyle habits and job continuation are linked together, giving a deeper understanding of the root cause and consequences of healthy living, and I wanted to share an excerpt of the discussion:

"Coach Collins, I know the fall season is a great time to get my coworkers motivated about implementing healthier lifestyle habits," Olivia shared.

An accountant for a local governmental agency, Olivia wanted her coworkers to explore their options for and focus their attention on eating healthier and exercising. To get them motivated, she asked me to come to their company for a get-fit stay-fit discussion. Olivia was excited about how small lifestyle changes had improved her blood pressure and blood cholesterol levels.

On the day of our meeting, Olivia introduced me to her coworkers, Valerie, the purchasing specialist, and Carol, a courts manager.

Disturbed by the events that led to the vacant office of a friend and coworker, Olivia stated, "Coach, one of our coworkers in the IT department was recently terminated. We're talking about someone who was praised throughout her tenure with the company for her outstanding contributions to IT implementations. She was considered one of the organization's most valued employees."

Carol interrupted and said, "Over the past three years, our friend had incurred multiple bouts with cancer. She was diagnosed with breast cancer in 2013 then lung cancer in 2014. She was eligible for and received the federally mandated twelve weeks of family and medical leave (FMLA). Based on our leave extended policy and her inability to return back to work, she received an additional ninety days of temporary disability leave. Later in 2014, she was diagnosed with brain cancer. Because she had exhausted all available leave options, she was terminated. Now, she's on COBRA having to pay over $600 a month for her medical insurance, a cost she cannot continue paying."

"The story of our friend is a sad and an unfortunate outcome, but it happens every day," Valerie said. "We all must face the reality that inactivity and a continuum of poor food choices like my mocha madness ice cream, two-piece fried chicken dinners, fried calamari, cheese ravioli, and blueberry muffins include ingredients that can result in health concerns sooner rather than later. A single parent of two small children, I can't afford to end up like our friend."

"The impact of poor health has become a major concern in organizations," I pointed out. "Employees who are not practicing healthy lifestyle habits and who fail to meet the company half way by taking advantage of its wellness tools and programs may be risking their jobs. I don't mean to imply that your coworker's situation was the result of unhealthy lifestyle habits, but we're all predisposed for disease and illness. In some cases, even when we're doing the right things (eating healthier, exercising, practicing self-care), we end up facing a major health concern, but in an effort to reap the benefits of a healthier lifestyle (better mood and energy levels, improved memory and brain health, heart health, digestive health, respiratory health, a healthy weight, strong bones, etc.), it's critical we commit to and practice healthy lifestyle habits."

WHAT ABOUT THE BUSINESS OWNER?

So you want to own your own business or you already own a business. As I interact more with small-business owners, I find that the reason for not incorporating healthier habits is no different than non-business owners. A primary statement is, "I don't have time." And my response is, "taking care of your business equals taking care of yourself."

Your business is synonymous with you. Just like you want a healthy and evolving business, you want a healthy and evolving you. You must take the necessary steps to foster a healthy, low-stress life. Those steps can include eating more fruits and vegetables to promote a healthy immune system, incorporating some form of physical activity to promote a healthy heart, and getting a good night's sleep to promote clear thinking, reduced stress, and a good mood. When your business is struggling and times are hard, that's when you need these healthy practices more than ever to ensure the decisions you make are done with clarity, decisiveness, and confidence.

Consider that when you become sick, so does your CEO, CFO, and sales and marketing team because all of those positions are *you*! Your business operations are impaired until you're up and running again. That impairment (its length depending on your situation) can cause you to lose potential clients, stifle your ability to manage a project, or secure that major business venture that was going to take your business to the next level. The stakes are high. Maybe you took out a second mortgage on your home to try to keep your business going, or you may have collaborated with others to borrow money, or you borrowed money from the government. Then you have to factor the things in your personal life (family, finances, and relationships).

Regardless of the size of your business and the level of responsibilities, your goal is the same. Even if you've been fiscally responsible, your daily thoughts and actions are focused on how to: enhance productivity, increase revenue, improve efficiency (cutting capital and operating costs), improve your customers' experience, increase your number of locations, and possibly move into global markets. In the midst of all of that are tough decisions, staff problems, etc.

More than likely, you didn't just wake up one day and say, "I'm going to start a business." Some planning had to occur. You started with a vision, set your goals, and developed your strategy and a systematic approach for achieving it. Living healthier is no different.

Whether you own a website design business, catering business, plumbing service, hair salon shop, tax preparation business, training company, or cleaning service, when you become sick with some illness, so do all the job roles you play in your business. You have to make YOU a priority because if you don't, you may impact the continuance of your business. Think about what you can do today to start the process of eating better, incorporating some form of physical activity into your daily routine, and what stress reduction exercises you can incorporate.

YOUR TURN-AROUND PLAN

What health and fitness goals do you want to achieve while under construction? What steps are you going to take to achieve them? Remember, if you're not taking care of your mind and body, all of those pursuits, ambitions, and activities you devise are in jeopardy. Before you chart the activities in your PPP, your moment of truth includes conducting a review of your current health and fitness state. These include questions like: What are you eating? Are you eating nutritious meals free from chemicals (artificial sweeteners, natural or artificial flavors, coloring agents, acids, preservatives)? Are you eating a wholesome breakfast every day? Are you drinking a sufficient amount of water? Are you getting the proper amount of sleep? Do you need to reduce your consumption of restaurant eating? Do you need to reduce your intake of alcohol consumption?

What simple exercise activity can you commit to doing for your turn-around plan? Can you walk in your neighborhood or your local park for fifteen minutes, four times a week?

I love what Ken shared about his running career.

> **Ken:** I learned early in my "running career" that I was not built for speed. However, winning a race or even placing in my age group was never that important. What was important was finishing the race. In my racing career of 1,178 races (as of May 22, 2021), I never had a DNF (did not finish). As I continued to run in my '70s, I realized that I may be serving as an inspiration to others. I remember running on the Sam Houston State University Campus

one day, and I passed a young lady. As I passed her, she said, "You have nice legs—for an old guy." At so many races, people come up to me after the race and tell me that they were trying to keep up with me the entire race. I do not know how many times a runner said to me, "I hope I'm still running when I am your age."

CAREER/BUSINESS

At some point, you must face your truth—your reality. Are you happy and fulfilled in your career? Do you long to be an entrepreneur where you work tirelessly to sustain a venture that you love and enjoy?

HOW ARE YOU PREPARING TO MOVE IN YOUR CAREER JOURNEY?

Companies are implementing hiring processes that position them to find the best of the best. Knowing that the right talent is critical as they are expanding and innovating, these companies are searching for creative minds and conscientious workers. Beyond the traditional criteria of education, certification, job history, and qualifications, they prioritize other factors such as past projects, experiences, and achievements.

Some workers have strengths that can be an asset for a company, are unique, and stand out. Your goal is to move through the hiring process from an applicant (someone who has applied for a position) to a candidate (someone who has been deemed qualified for the position). Once you get to the candidate stage, the company's hiring process may very well include the utilization of assessments, which obtain objective insight into the skill and personality of a candidate.

During a conversation with a friend who works for a major transportation company, we talked about turnover issues her company was experiencing. I asked her why their employees were leaving the company, and she shared three primary reasons: Employees who believed they could handle the physical demands of the job but couldn't. Employees who were hired as part time and left the company for full-time employment. She then spoke about leadership and communication styles, sharing how older supervisors with tenure were burnt out and bitter. They had checked out, not involving themselves with or supporting their employees. She talked about their younger supervisors who yelled and screamed at team members. I asked her about a specific example, and she told me about an employee's responsibility to load a plane. The supervisor yelled, saying, "What part of now don't you understand? Get over here!"

We talked about targeted training for front-line leaders, such as coaching scenarios and how to communicate with team members. When I asked about their recruitment of employees, she spoke of transformation in the hiring process and how it required passing assessments. She told of two hundred applicants who filled out an application, completed the assessment, and passed the assessment. Of the 200 applicants, 123 failed the assessment.

Are you ready for the possible assessment test? An example of such a test would be a situational assessment, which analyzes behavior through a series of proposed scenarios. In this particular test, one is given an incident describing a workplace conflict, and the candidate chooses which course of action is most correct. The company utilizes the assessment to understand how a candidate would work with teams and fit in with the work environment.

Are you ready for the personality test? In the earlier chapters, you read about the right state of mind and personal core values. Here we go. The personality traits of an individual, including their beliefs, the motivation driving them, and the disposition they possess usually play a considerable role in their performance on the job. There are several different personality tests that can help measure how well you will perform at the organization based on your interpersonal skills, the motivation and ambition that drive you, and the role that you can excel in due to your behavioral traits. The company utilizes personality tests to help in analyzing if you are a good fit for its team and its work environment.

Are you ready for the chemistry test? Typically, we think of chemistry when it comes to dating and marriage, but some companies may begin testing for workplace chemistry. It's talked about in acting—the audition that is a chemistry read designed to determine how two actors will work together. When watching a professional sporting event or listening to sports analysts, there's typically a discussion about a team's chemistry. They will talk about players who have great chemistry together, are present for each other, focused on each other, honest with each other, open with each other, accountable to each other, and supportive of each other. This is all to reach a common goal instead of selfish pursuits.

Tons of resources on the Internet show how to prepare and pass these types of tests, so prepare to MOVE in your career journey by starting your research today.

USE YOUR TIME WISELY. DON'T TAKE TIME FOR GRANTED.

In the world of professional sports, when the head coach doesn't deliver a national championship over a period of time, he or she is let go. The days where a leader stays with an organization and doesn't deliver next-level results or growth are diminishing. Corporations traditionally have had a professional sports' "let go" mind set, but now it's in companies and local and state governmental agencies.

Companies and organizations are looking for their leaders and employees to be active go-getters. Are you a go-getter in your company or in your organization? Think about a political candidate who has convinced voters of why they're the best candidate for the role. How would you respond to the following questions? What is your track record with the company or in an organization? How have you delivered? How have you individually, and as a team contributor, accomplished? The bottom line is: How have you demonstrated your value to the people who have a say in your continued or upward movement within the company or organization?

We all think at some point that we're ready for the next-level position in the company or organization. Maybe it's because you have twenty years of work experience. Maybe it's because you've gone back to school and obtained an advanced degree. Maybe it's because you've obtained an industry-recognized certification.

Demonstrating your value to management begins with your work experience, education, and certifications, but work experience alone will no longer suffice. Educational pursuits, achievements, and knowledge alone will no longer suffice. Companies and organizations are looking for all three. While talking to a young man who had recently received his Project Management Certifications (PMC), he was excited about the career doors the certification would open. I explained that the certification gave him the knowledge of understanding, which was acquired through a variety of methods such as explanation, observation, research, and reading books, but those skills are acquired by doing. Just because he had the knowledge, it didn't translate into him being able to do it. I explained to the young man that the best way to master something is through regular practice or trial and error. His skill-based learning seeks to build upon knowledge by developing practical expertise in a specific area. I gave him the following example:

An electrician requires the background knowledge of terms, such as alternating current (AC), direct current (DC), fuse, load, parallel circuit, series circuit, short circuit, conductor, generator, insulator, power and watts, voltage and volts, and many more terms. While in school, the electrician student puts this knowledge to use by obtaining hands-on experience with circuits, tools, measurements, conduit bending, and more. This leads to the electrician student building circuits, wire rooms, and troubleshooting electrical problems.

As evident by the example, having knowledge about something does not make a person skilled in it—and equally, being skilled at something does not mean you have all the required knowledge to stand out while doing it. Don't get me wrong, knowledge is good, but applying the knowledge builds the proficiency to make a difference.

Remember the EEOC situation I shared with you in Chapter 2? I talked about what I did afterward and how I started researching and gathering resources to increase my knowledge and facilitate my technical knowledge about the critical area. My knowledge enhanced the analytical, research, communication, interview, critical-thinking, problem-solving, and writing skills necessary to conduct EEOC investigations.

Upward movement occurs with the extras you've contributed to the growth and success of the company or organization. To stand out among your colleagues and subordinates, you must do more than your job. You have to continuously invest your time and resources to learn and do more with what you learn, so you can be more.

For the employee who talks about applying for multiple promotional opportunities within their organization, I would ask that person about the contributions they've made outside of their assigned responsibilities to make their department/organization better and more successful. How have you made your own job better? Have you led a special project? Do you respectfully share ideas with management about your job responsibilities and how they can be completed more efficiently? Have you facilitated process improvement changes or developed a departmental standard operating procedure or a training manual? These are only some of the ways you can make the greatest use of your time.

BE READY TO TAKE THE KEYS TO DRIVE

When the keys to drive the show are given to you, make sure you're prepared and ready to move forward. One day while driving and listening to talk radio, the radio personality talked about struggles companies had finding good people. He spoke about his show sponsors and friends from various industries—restaurant, technology, retail, transportation, oil, and gas—being despondent about talent pools.

Even if you don't get the promotion you're seeking within your current organization, when you commit to learning and doing more with what you learn, you better equip yourself with the knowledge, skills, and talents to present a next-level you to your next employer. Just make sure you are ready and have got your BEs in order: Be a unifier, contributor, influencer, supporter, transformer, deliverer, innovator, crisis manager, problem-solver, wise money manager, and a grateful person.

NOT YOUR TIME YET?

The truth may be that it's not your time for upward or outward movement regarding your career. During those times, I was unhappy, unfulfilled, and undervalued in my current situation, I found solace in my volunteerism. I said solace, but it was really joy. I used my skills and talents to positively impact people, developing, planning, and delivering job readiness training classes at my church. I planned and led fitness classes at my church, and I conducted lifestyle education classes for organizations like the Greater Southwest Black Chamber of Commerce during the time I served as a board member. The best distractions you can have are the activities that help others advance their goals. Organizations like your local church are always looking for people to participate in volunteer initiatives.

In the process of using my skills and talents, I also enhanced my skills and talents. Whether by volunteering for a civic, charitable, or humanitarian organization, there is always something to learn. Volunteer work can broaden your experience, exposure, knowledge, and skills as you communicate with patrons and sponsors, plan and prioritize assignments, write reports, work in a team, solve problems, adapt to changes, practice time management, and so on. This is all being done as you are probably doing something different, learning about a new industry, exploring interests and passions, and giving back to your community.

When I embarked on my journey to be an actor some years ago, I heard others in the acting world talk about attending film festivals. I thought of how nice it would be to attend a film festival, so I did some research on film festivals coming to Texas. In 2018, I discovered the National Black Film Festival was coming to town, and I visited their website, noticing they were looking for volunteers. It was a perfect opportunity to further explore my acting interest. I could volunteer, attend some of the workshops, increase my knowledge about the industry, and build my acting network—all for the price of donating my time.

Is there any knowledge you want to acquire in particular? What information and skills will you need to have in order to achieve your career or business goals? Is there a volunteer opportunity you can research to help you achieve your passions and interests?

What level do you want to reach in your career to assume a leadership role or earn a degree, advanced degree, or certification to improve your networking skills or start your own business?

I love what Tony shared in his book,

> "In my early thirties, I realized that my corporate career would be short lived. So, I used my time in corporate America to learn as much as possible from other executives about their decision-making process, especially in sales, marketing, and procurement, so I could apply this toward running my own business.
>
> My advice to any employee is to assume you'll be laid off tomorrow. You're just an employee number and will be easily replaced, so always be prepared for the worst."

There are things you have no control over, such as getting the job you applied for if it's not your time, but you can take seriously what you do have control over. These are things like preparing for the interview, researching the company, knowing the organizational structure, dressing appropriately, practicing for the interview, making copies of your resume, and making sure there are no misspellings or grammatical errors.

Chart your career path! If at first you do not succeed, try, try again! Never give up on your pursuits, and always seek to A.C.C.O.M.P.L.I.S.H.

Aspire to

Create a path to

Chart your future by

Organizing and

Managing your life, so you can

Prioritize how you will

Learn and

Implement a

Strategy that will

Heighten your opportunities for a satisfying and successful career journey.

COMMUNITY

Do you want to make a difference in your community or the world? If so, how? We all have a part to play when investing in our communities. It starts with being passionate about something, which leads to purpose. That passion might stem from something that affected you in your childhood or your adulthood, such as alcohol or drug addiction, homelessness, battered women, domestic violence, child abuse, a drunk driver, financial literacy, or a food bank. It could be something you've become interested in, like social justice, criminal justice, climate control, health, or fitness. The point is to get involved, volunteer, contribute to making a difference, and commit to sharing your ideas, gifts, and talents. A great place to start is your church, and beyond that, there are literally hundreds of non-profit/charitable organizations always looking for helpers. It's a great way to use your gifts and talents to serve and teach others.

When I think about the hundreds of non-profit/charitable organizations, I know quite often it is the result of circumstances that led the person or group to create it because of something that has impacted their life. They created the non-profits to help raise awareness for things like an adult sibling who had a disability or might have been born deaf, suffered an accident that resulted in amputation, a spouse who was diagnosed with ALS, a child who committed suicide, a spouse who killed someone while under the influence, a relative who became homeless, a mother who was a victim of domestic violence, a parent who was stricken with Dementia, a child with autism, a friend who grappled with paying the high cost of health care, a relative who was killed by a drunk driver, a relative who suffered from mental illness, a parent whose child was killed by a police officer, a parent killed by a hit-and-run driver, or the sole supporter of the family.

Experiences provoke all of us to be a part of the movements and organizations that seek to engage, educate, empower, and exalt. One of the best examples I read about was someone who opened a movie theatre and hired people with disabilities like Down syndrome. Who knows? You, too, may have the formation of a non-profit circulating in your head. It may have impacted your life such that you want to create or share awareness from a different perspective. You'll find that you're not the only one who has experienced it. You may be the catalyst for getting others involved to help bring awareness and provide resources for protection or prevention.

When it comes to building cohesive, collaborative, and caring teams at work, you'll find companies using volunteerism as a mechanism for such. The company business—its products and services are paramount! But in addition to company business, research was shown that employees who volunteer with their company are fulfilled knowing they made a difference to a special cause. As you, the titled or untitled leader of the team, work to build cohesive, collaborative, and caring relationships among your team members, don't forget about non-profit volunteer activities as an option. There may be an opportunity to walk for an employee's child who has been diagnosed with leukemia. Nothing builds a team better than team involvement on a joint effort.

Your community involvement just might contribute to your best experiences. I remember two specific times where my volunteerism contributed to me having fun. In 2017, I was blessed with the opportunity to volunteer for the Houston Super Bowl Host Committee for Super Bowl LI (51) held in Houston, Texas. It was an amazing experience.

Early on, I got to work as a volunteer interviewer at the volunteer headquarters. During my volunteer stint, the host committee reinforced at every opportunity that its mission was to give everyone an unparalleled Super Bowl experience. For months, the volunteers were hailed as super stars. As a volunteer, you never felt anything less than a super star. The host committee knew if the volunteers felt and believed they were super stars, then everyone they interacted with would receive the super star treatment.

One of my bucket list items for years was to attend an in-person Super Bowl game. Always hearing about how expensive it was, I didn't know if/when that bucket list item would ever come to fruition. In 2017, it did. As a result of my volunteerism throughout the NFL Experience and other events, I was selected to be a game-day volunteer at NRG. Little did I know I'd eventually end up in the Verizon suite at NRG watching the Super Bowl game. The point is that you never know how giving your time to make a difference to your community may boomerang back to you.

LEISURE/FUN

When was the last time you did something for the first time? Two things can happen because of firsts. First, your firsts may become your passion and lead to a new hobby or career pursuit. Second, your firsts may serve to foster conversations about relatable experiences while on your job, in your career, or as a business owner.

A great way to keep your life fun and interesting is to always pursue firsts. If you're wondering what I mean when I say firsts, I mean to move outside of your comfort zone, to move outside of your self-imposed box of limits, to try new things, and to exert the energy while creating and pursuing new experiences for yourself and your family. When my family and friends were new parents, I'd love to hear them talk about the firsts of their baby—first bath, first smile, first laugh, first word, first tooth, first step, first birthday, and first Christmas. As their baby advanced to being a toddler, tween, and teenager to a young adult, there were many more firsts, like first Easter speech, first day of school, first swim lesson, first bike ride, first sport's practice, first recital, first win, first driver's license, first voter's registration card, and first day of college tour. There are too many firsts to list, but the point is that you can hear the excitement in their voices through the telephone—in the days before social media—as they recap watching their baby through young adulthood experience things for the first time.

As people get older, the consideration of firsts seems to diminish. Maybe it's because of their consumption with life's obligations and responsibilities. Whatever the case, people are less motivated to experience firsts when they get older, and it's not because the first-time opportunities do not exist. I think they are simply living comfortably without the initiative to live life to the fullest in a meaningful and memorable way—a life filled with fun, excitement, and adventure. Sure, people talk about having a bucket list, but they never pursue the activities related to their bucket list. I talked earlier about my bucket list item to attend a Super Bowl game, and it was definitely one of my best first experiences. The pursuit of firsts keeps us smiling, laughing, and in some cases, experiencing things we thought we'd never do.

For years my mother would talk about her desire to visit the New England states. So, for her seventieth birthday, I made sure her desire became a reality. In 2011, we flew from Houston, Texas to Manchester, New Hampshire and rented a car to begin our five-day New England Tour. She had one of her life's best experiences as we visited various parts of the region. New Hampshire (The Flume Gorge and White Mountains) and Massachusetts (Boston, Martha's Vineyard, and Hyannis Port to Yarmouth in Cape Cod).

It is never too late to pursue your thoughts and visions of fun, adventure, and leisure. Don't wait, hesitate, or procrastinate. There is no time like the present to start. You're never too old to learn how to swim, play tennis, train for a 5K or half-marathon, write a book, make wine from scratch, plan an event, present a workshop, ride a horse, design fashion, play a musical instrument, or be a better writer. I know you have a lot of thoughts circulating in your head. Yes, I know you're in your forties, fifties, sixties, and seventies. You hear people talk about things they've done, and you think, *I'm scared to do that, I missed out on doing that,* and *I'm too old now.* I thought I'd provide a list of firsts for you to consider at your age. They can also serve as firsts not just for you, but you and your spouse/partner, you and your children, or you and your family members. Check them out below. They are:

- first volunteer assignment;
- first group fitness class;
- first photography class;
- first computer class;
- first foreign (e.g., Spanish, French, etc.) language class;
- first writer's workshop;
- first book to read;
- first conference, workshop, or seminar;
- first in-person football, basketball, baseball, or soccer game;
- first 5K walk as a participant;
- first pickleball game as a participant;
- first road trip;
- first airplane ride;
- first solo vacation trip;
- first walk on the beach;
- first camping trip;
- first cruise;
- first jet-skiing, snorkeling, and/or parasailing adventure;
- first trip out of the country;
- first trip to an amusement park;

- first dance class;

- first painting class;

- first cooking class;

- first acting class;

- first chess game;

- first card game;

- first trip to a winery;

- first hiking trip;

- first landscaping or gardening class;

- first do-it-yourself project;

- first arts and crafts class;

- first make-up application class;

- first trip to an antique store;

- first trip to an art gallery;

- first trip to the zoo;

- first trip to an aquarium; and

- first trip to visit the Smithsonian Institution.

I often hear people say, "Life is an adventure." I sometimes hear someone refer to someone else's life by saying, "She's living her best life." I wonder about what that really means to those people. Is it because the referenced person has acquired some perceived belief of wealth? Or is it because the referenced person travels extensively? I'll hear people say, "I'm living vicariously through you." Stop it. Start experiencing life through your own lens and your own experiences. People often share with me things other people are doing. My response is, "That's great! Love it!" But unlike the person, I don't stay stuck on what someone is doing. The only thing I want to be stuck on is what I'm doing. Don't be content watching other people do. You can do as well. There's enough room for all of us to do.

Don't be discouraged by the naysayers who say, "Aren't you too old to be doing that?" Make sure you don't put stock in others' opinions of what your interests are—that is, don't let any negative feedback affect your enjoyment of whatever you choose to pursue in your individual firsts. I ran my first marathon at the age of thirty-four. I remember an ex-boyfriend saying to me, "Aren't you too old to be running?" Well, as I stated before, I've run eighteen marathons and thirty-plus half-marathons since my first. Twenty-plus years, and as I still participate in races, my dad will say, "You're old now. You need to stop that running. When you get my age you won't be able to walk."

I smile and think how blessed I am to have benchmarks like Ken, who—at the time of me writing this book—is eighty years of age and still participating in races.

Now, if you're someone who prefers to have someone alongside you, but no one you know shares your interests, settle on the fact that it will be a solo adventure. Simply research the numerous platforms that connect people with similar interests. Are you a woman who's interested in hiking? Find a women's hiking group to join. Are you interested in making a quilt of your running shirts? Find a quilting class in your area. Are you interested in restoring a classic car? Find a trade school you can attend.

When you look at life from a different perspective, the possibilities are endless. You'll just need to tap into your confidence of ability, growth potential, and evolution to put in the work, and when you do, you'll want to seize the opportunities that come your way. You'll want to exert the energy needed to do the things you want to experience, like research, prepare, plan, explore, create, act, evolve, and question. What is a first you will now create for yourself?

THE IMPACT ON YOUR PROFESSIONAL LIFE

You will be a better listener, sharer, connector, and supporter. Your ability to create collaborative, meaningful, memorable, and productive work environments will lead to enhanced workplace relationships and opportunities.

Attitude is everything. I can't say it enough. Treat others the way you want to be treated—with respect, kindness, and compassion.

Think about a situation in your professional life when you reacted and communicated defensively. What did the other person say that provoked your defensiveness? How did their words make you feel? What assumptions or judgments about the other person's intentions or motives—or judgments about the person (i.e., selfish, inconsiderate, rude, controlling, mean-spirited)—did you make? What did you say in response? What underlying perceptions, concerns, needs, fears, or vulnerabilities were at the root of your reaction? What triggered your reaction? What was the outcome of the defensive encounter?

Is any part of your mindset holding you back? Is there any part of the way you behave that concerns you, such as always agitated, anxious, or depressed? Why? Some possible reasons for a bad attitude might be obesity, arthritis affecting your quality of life, cancer, medical bills, job loss, repossession, bankruptcy, divorce, or breakup. There are so many reasons to go under construction to be a better you—mind, body, and spirit—a better leader to yourself, and a better leader to those within your circle of influence and responsibility.

You don't have to be the smartest and most intelligent in the room, but you do need to have the right attitude. Always display a good attitude. Do not be the employee who is rude, vain, critical, shows up late to work and/or meetings, does not take responsibility, and blames others for their mistakes. Always be kind to those around you. Sometimes the most unlikely person can become your boss.

Whether you are interacting with a happy, jovial, unhappy, irrational, angry, or upset customer, your approach, attitude, and response should always be the same. Begin with a smile, extend a welcome, assist the customer with his or her needs, and thank the customer for the opportunity to serve and/or address his or her needs. I shared with you earlier that one of my favorite things to do is write while eating breakfast and drinking coffee at my favorite restaurant. During one of my visits (around 7:30 a.m.), I noticed a new lady in training taking orders and operating the terminal. While giving my order to the new lady, I commented to the cashier I was familiar with that she was training someone new. She smiled and said, "Yes." The new lady never smiled. As I was getting my coffee, I noticed the new lady's lack of expression as she interacted with others behind me.

When I saw the lady I was familiar with on another day, I commented to her that the new lady didn't seem to be excited about training. The lady commented, "I don't think she's a morning person." I noticed the new lady had been moved to a new area. She was in the food area, cutting an assortment of fresh fruit and separating and placing the fruit pieces into bins. I'm sure the leader of the restaurant recognized the cashier role was not a good fit for the lady and placed her in a more suitable area. I applaud the leader for making that decision. Unfortunately, some leaders may not react the same by moving an employee.

As shown with the lady, an attitude can have an impact on a person's job and will oftentimes directly correlate with their interactions in the workplace. When you think back and assess how you'll empower, enlighten, and encourage others within your circle of influence (e.g., kids, siblings, coworkers, etc.), make sure you think legacy. Live with no regrets and carry no shame or guilt as you make the best possible impact within your personal and professional life.

Rest Stop Exercise #10

A BE to Remember: Be Truthful.

Being truthful will ensure you realistically plan your next-level pursuit of personal and professional endeavors and relationships.

M O V E

Master **Omit** **Visualize** **Execute**

What in your "right now" do you need to master to ensure you're being truthful when assessing your thoughts, feelings, and actions?

PERSONAL

_____

_____

_____

_____

_____

_____

_____

PROFESSIONAL

_____

_____

_____

_____

_____

_____

_____

What unwanted passengers do you need to omit?

PERSONAL

_____

_____

_____

_____

_____

_____

PROFESSIONAL

_____

_____

_____

_____

_____

_____

What action activities do you visualize?

PERSONAL

_____

_____

_____

_____

_____

_____

PROFESSIONAL

_____

_____

_____

_____

_____

_____

How will you execute your action plan?

PERSONAL

_____

_____

_____

_____

_____

_____

PROFESSIONAL

_____

_____

_____

_____

_____

_____

NOTES

Chapter 11

Wearing Your Ear Plugs During Your Planning Phase

Not everything that is faced can be changed. But nothing can be changed until it is faced.

—James A. Baldwin

When I get local or out-of-town acting opportunities, I always have to drive somewhere new to get to the filming location. Unfortunately for me, the navigation system in my car is outdated due to its age. Rather than waiting to use some GPS driving app on my cellular telephone the day of, I use my computer the day before to enter the start and end addresses, and I map out the route I'll take ahead of time. I study the route and make sure I have a good idea of my driving route. I pay close attention to landmarks identified on the route, remembering where and when I'll access highways and byways and make turns on streets and roads. Simply put, I block out the noise to effectively analyze and outline my driving plan.

A call to action! There have been many points about goals, plans, purpose, passion, targets, strategies, and priorities to provoke a perspective and initiative to MOVE. Being intentional with your PPP is a great starting place, but it won't ensure success. Your PPP simply seeks to serve as a guide and focus your attention on what's necessary to achieve results, which can lead to you being a better you.

So many people want to do the right thing, but life's obligations, pursuits, challenges, and distractions always seem to take priority. If you are serious about addressing your "Now what?," then a good start is to set some goals. Goals are the underlying building blocks of achievement, not just on our jobs, in our spiritual life, in our relationships, or in our personal finances, but in every aspect of our lives. They will provide direction and the framework for fulfilling your desires.

You have the power to be a better version and leader of yourself. All you need is purpose, a plan—plot your navigation—to make the best decisions, and to exert the effort to make your dreams, desires, hopes, and ambitions a reality. With power, love, and faith, you can achieve.

For my 2020 birthday, I traveled with one of my running friends to the Bahamas and ran in the Marathon Bahamas. One of the most exciting features of the marathon was that it ended at the oceanfront at Arawak Cay. For months, I had viewed social media posts of previous Marathon Bahamas finishers getting into the ocean as a celebratory act, and I knew I wanted to do the same. After my marathon finish, I walked into the ocean waters, excited about my opportunity to celebrate in the beautiful blue Bahamian water. There were waves, but they appeared calm. There was no indication of anything hazardous in the waters.

While standing waist-deep in the ocean and trying to encourage my running partner to join me, a force of water swept my feet from under me, causing me to fall backward. The waters pulled me away from the shore. My friend yelled for me to remain calm and move in the direction of the water. As I repeatedly attempted to move forward, the waters pushed me backward. I had gotten caught up in a rip current. During the ordeal, my friend focused my attention on not panicking and not fighting the waters. The blessing is that I eventually escaped a frightening situation by going a different direction to get out of the current. Did I mention that I can't swim?

The whole ordeal was a reminder of how circumstances can change in an instant and how we should act logically to escape something trying to trap us.

Below are some starters you may generate from your PPP to facilitate your clearing away process and plot your navigation to create goals for yourself:

- Reflect! Spend a portion of your weekend reflecting on you, your work environment, your actions/behaviors in the workplace, and your ideal work environment.

- Journal! Articulate your thoughts on paper. Writing it down makes your beliefs and desires plain, along with where you want to be, what you want to achieve, and what you need to do.

- Share it! Acquire a mentor, life coach, or professional who can help you identify strategic steps for moving forward and achieving your next level.

- Plan something new! Take a class to learn a new skill, enroll in a fitness program, take a road trip, attend a career-enhancing conference, or volunteer.

Before you get started, I wanted to share a list of BEs to consider:

- BE okay with brokenness.
- BE financially independent.

- BE pilot-like in clearing yourself for take-off.
- BE ready to change.
- BE in conversation with yourself.
- BE confident.
- BE okay with starting over.
- BE in competition with yourself.
- BE open to what's necessary for success.
- BE supportive of others and their endeavors.
- BE committed to sharing your exes to help others escape.
- BE legacy driven.
- BE a difference-maker.

YOUR "UNDER-CONSTRUCTION" PERSONAL PROJECT PLAN (PPP)

You've been driving around now for quite some time. You've completed several exercises to help you better analyze and identify changes you can make to be a better version of yourself. I hope these exercises also provoked thought on how to get unstuck and move your life forward.

What have you learned about yourself that you are positively committed to improving? Take a moment and jot down five things.

_____

_____

_____

_____

_____

Just know you have to practice being better. I know all of BEs I want to be take practice. I especially stay in practice mode trying to be better in the following areas: active listening, empathy, critical thinking, positive work usage, etcetera.

In earlier chapters, I shared stories about encounters I had while writing at a favorite restaurant. Here's one more that happened while I was finishing up the book because it really highlights how the opportunity to practice being a better version of yourself can come from anywhere in your daily life. During another visit to my favorite restaurant, I observed a young male approach two ladies sitting at a booth in front of the booth where I was sitting. I couldn't hear clearly what he said to them, but I could discern he was asking for money. After listening to whatever story he told them, the ladies reached into their purses and handed him some money. While observing his interaction with the ladies, I figured I might be next and, because I didn't have any cash money, I decided I would get him something to eat.

After looking around at the other patrons, the young male noticed an older man sitting alone and went there next to give what I assumed was the same spiel. After listening, the older man asked him a series of questions. He asked his name, and they both exchanged names. Then he asked about the young man's goals. Now imagine me with a surprised facial expression, because I thought it was an odd next question for a stranger. The young man responded, "Having a family." The older man redirected the question about goals and asked him about his job goals. The young man said, "I thought about being an EMT, but I have medical constraints." The older man asked about what it took to become an EMT. I could tell the young man didn't know and imagined the older man knew what he wanted to achieve would take several minutes because after a short pause, he offered to buy the young man something to eat, walked with him to the counter, and ordered him a breakfast sandwich. Upon their return to the older man's table, the older man went into a long discussion about goals and doing the necessary research. He directed the young man to go to the local community college to get information about becoming an EMT.

Because I could discern the young male may have had some special needs, I walked over to their table and asked if I could interrupt. Of course, they allowed me to do so. I suggested the older man do a search for Goodwill Industries for the young man and explained that the organization has training and career advancement programs. Both men acknowledged they were familiar with the organization, so I returned back to my table.

The older man asked the young man about the last time he had worked. The young man replied, "2018." He asked the young man about what he had been doing since then, to which the young man replied, "Just walking around." When he asked the young man about jobs he had applied for, the young man provided a story. He then asked the young man about his living arrangements. The young man talked about living with friends here and there and staying with his mother here and there. The older man explained to him that his situation may be more difficult than others, but that he could achieve his goals with the right actions. He went as far as to remind the young man that he already had a goal for that morning—to get up, get dressed, and walk to the restaurant to ask for money.

After listening to the conversation, I felt bad that all I'd wanted to do was buy the young man a meal. The guidance and insight the older man gave was so much more valuable. For me, the older man was a great reminder to always practice doing more to be empathetic, to engage, encourage, empower, and truly help someone improve their life.

Now it's time for you to plan and act. I know there are many plans online to help with personal and professional development, and they are good ones. You don't have to re-invent the wheel. You may decide to modify it to fit what you value most in your life. For now, I just want you to focus on activities you can start to move forward. When you finish reading this book, you will have completed twelve exercises to provoke things you can master, omit, visualize, and execute.

Consider the PPP worksheets in the Your Under-Construction Worksheets section—your road map for moving your life to the next level—and begin to create your "under-construction" personal project plan.

Rest Stop Exercise #11

A BE to Remember: Be Solution-Oriented.

The solution for resolution is the development of your "under-construction" personal project plan to reconcile and heal your wounds.

M   O   V   E

Master   **Omit**   **Visualize**   **Execute**

What in your "right now" do you need to master the sources and resources you'll need to plan and execute your PPP?

PERSONAL

_____

_____

_____

_____

_____

_____

PROFESSIONAL

_____

_____

_____

_____

_____

_____

What unwanted passengers do you need to omit?

PERSONAL

_____

_____

_____

_____

_____

_____

_____

PROFESSIONAL

_____

_____

_____

_____

_____

_____

_____

What action activities do you visualize?

PERSONAL

_____

_____

_____

_____

_____

_____

_____

PROFESSIONAL

_____

_____

_____

_____

_____

_____

_____

How will you execute your action plan?

PERSONAL

_____

_____

_____

_____

_____

_____

PROFESSIONAL

_____

_____

_____

_____

_____

_____

Chapter 12

Reaching the End of Your Legacy Construction

Every human being is under construction from conception to death.

—Billy Graham

I know you're excited about the completion of your "under-construction" personal project plan. You've made some major improvements to be a better version of yourself. It's time to celebrate you.

Let's recap your achievements. You've shifted lanes of perspectives, constructed some drainage work to clear your state of mind, repaved your core values, removed objects affecting your choices, installed new entry and exit ramps, added paths to meet new people, widened byways of gratitude, included a multi-use bridge to connect with others, created freedom access roads, tore down some concrete walls to get to the truth, installed some sound barriers, and now you're adding new signage.

Congratulations on your new physical customized road signs representing your "right now." The messages are beautiful. "New Road Layout Ahead." "Wrong Way." "One Way." "New Traffic Path Ahead." "Exit Do Not Enter." "No U-Turn." "Welcome to Passion, Purpose, and Joy."

FROM CONCEPTION TO DEATH

The road of life is not infinite. Our journey traveled on Earth will end.

When you think about your journey to legacy, it's simple. Live the narrative you want to represent your life. The narrative we live will determine if we leave a meaningful and memorable legacy. A good question to ask yourself is, "What influence do I want to have on others when my life on Earth has ended?"

Before I really understood the meaning of legacy, I thought it was about people who had a building, ward of a hospital, or highway named after them. I thought it was about people who left huge endowments to universities. I thought it was about wealthy people who made large financial donations to special causes. I thought it was people like a civil rights activist, a world religious leader, or a sports figure who opens a school for the disadvantaged. Then I came to the understanding that legacy wasn't about namesakes or wealth. A legacy is about all of us using our talents and resources in positive, meaningful, and memorable ways to benefit others through our beliefs, values, passion, purpose, and pursuits—all of which will birth influence and leave a lasting impact.

So, live the narrative you want to be your legacy, and your legacy will be representative of how you live. Live your life in the way you want others to share your influential and meaningful stories. Live in a way that your gains don't unravel or disappear.

I asked Ken about why he co-founded the Seven Hills Running Club in 1985. He stated, "The club was formed to promote running as a means of achieving and maintaining physical fitness in Huntsville and its surrounding communities. There was no running club in Huntsville when I moved to the city in 1985. While I was still new to the sport and had experience with the Rose /Runners Club in Tyler, it seemed like a good idea to form a new club. My secretary at the time, Cheryl Sewell—also a runner—agreed with me, and we formed the club. We had strong support from several other runners."

I asked Tony why he co-founded the National Black Marathoners Association in 2004. He stated, "The NBMA was created to award college scholarships to distance runners, to provide a venue for Black runners to meet, and to recognize the accomplishments of Black distance runners. We realized that new or prospective runners needed Black role models to help provide motivation. We also realized that the accomplishments of Black runners had been overlooked or ignored by the White running community. Thus, we created the National Black Distance Running Hall of Fame to highlight the achievements of Black runners, coaches, race directors, and others."

I'm a sports fanatic. One thing I love at the end of a game is to listen to the sports commentator or analyst talk about why a team lost the game. A comment that I hear most often is, "They would have won, but they ran out of time."

We all must prioritize who and what is important during our lives. During the COVID-19 pandemic throughout the year of 2020, many of my family and friends lost family and friends—totally unforeseen and unexpected deaths due to something that emerged out of nowhere. As a fitness and running coach, it was the day when a friend called me to share his heartache over the deaths of two male childhood friends within a two-month time period that saddened me even more. He shared that the first childhood friend (age fifty-four) died as the result of a stroke, and the second one (age fifty-eight) as the result of a heart attack. Both deaths had been totally unforeseen and unexpected. Both were married and had children. He talked about his friends and their lifestyle habits. People who—at the end of their workday—went home, grabbed an alcoholic beverage, and sat in their chair for the remainder of the day. He recounted that his friends never ate healthily, never exercised, and they never went to the doctor for their annual checkups.

You want to make sure you leave a legacy in which your journey is worth tracing.

- What will your journey say about you?
- What meaningful and memorable images will others have of you?
  - ➢ You planned ahead.
  - ➢ You prepared yourself.
  - ➢ You prepared your family.
  - ➢ You made good decisions.
  - ➢ You were a follower.
  - ➢ You were a leader.
  - ➢ You were an achiever.
  - ➢ You acknowledged your mistakes.
  - ➢ You had courage.
  - ➢ You believed in yourself.
  - ➢ You never gave up.
  - ➢ You loved yourself.
  - ➢ You loved others.

Write the stories for your book of life with passion, purpose, and intention. As we've talked about, you have to look back in order to move forward into the future. You want to retrace your steps. You want to remind yourself of the roads you've taken.

I pray your book of life includes many chapters, and I hope that your chapters include tales about the wonderful people who contributed to the exposure and experiences on your journeys. Include stories about the highs and lows, trials and errors, challenges and uncertainties, and delays and disappointments that contributed to your evolution and gains. This is useful and meaningful information to inspire and empower those who have and will cross your path. These are ways you chose to share and understand the perspective and uniqueness of others who crossed your path in their struggles, challenges, hurt, disappointment, and brokenness. This is how you pursued your dreams, ideas, and visions in the midst of it.

I pray the stories that make up the chapters in your book of life, which depicts your truths, will be a catalyst for transforming and celebrating love, peace, acceptance, and goodness for all of humanity.

I know you've heard this statement before, but there are two things in life that are for certain: death and taxes. So, why not make the most of your life while you're on Earth? Don't let your past create a narrative you can't escape. Be committed to pursuing and living a life that matters—one that is filled with peace, joy, health, happiness, passion, purpose, and fulfillment.

Your "under-construction" PPP will help you chart the course of the roads you want to improve—the roads that will include how you control the way you think, feel, act, and interact with others.

Make the difference on Earth you were created to make, and always remember: If you don't chart your legacy, someone else will.

Start living the legacy you want to leave. Your life. Your legacy. I can't wait to hear about the fruits of your "Now what?"

Rest Stop Exercise #12

A BE to Remember: Be Selfish.

Always be in pursuit of reconciling matters that help you better refine yourself and position you to be a better leader to yourself. It all starts with a point of critical self-reflection and self-analysis.

M O V E

Master **Omit** **Visualize** **Execute**

What in your "right now" do you need to master to live the legacy you want to leave?

PERSONAL

_____

_____

_____

_____

_____

_____

PROFESSIONAL

_____

_____

_____

_____

_____

_____

What unwanted passengers do you need to omit?

PERSONAL

_____

_____

_____

_____

_____

_____

_____

PROFESSIONAL

_____

_____

_____

_____

_____

_____

_____

What action activities do you visualize to help you
make better choices or enhanced choices?

PERSONAL

_____

_____

_____

_____

_____

_____

PROFESSIONAL

_____

_____

_____

_____

_____

_____

How will you execute your action plan?

PERSONAL

_____

_____

_____

_____

_____

_____

PROFESSIONAL

_____

_____

_____

_____

_____

_____

Join Bridgette's Roadworkers Community

Bridgette is committed to helping her roadworkers community members acknowledge their "right now," understand their purpose, and pursue being better in all aspects of their lives.

When you sign up, Bridgette will give you a free five-minute talk to get you started on your "under-construction" personal project plan (PPP).

Sign up by visiting http://www.yesiamfedup.com/
or send an email to hello@yesiamfedup.com and include
"free five-minute talk" in the subject line.

Need a Yes! I CAN MOVE Development and Coaching Program?

EMPLOYEE DEVELOPMENT AND COACHING

The Yes! I CAN MOVE Development and Coaching Program focuses on various aspects of developing employees and achieving optimal performance from your team members through one-on-one talks. Course content includes the following:

- Coaching to MOVE Relationships Forward
- The Soft Skills That Matter
- Securing a Customer-Focused Commitment
- Why Celebratory Conversations Matter

SPEAKING SERVICES

Get and keep your group engaged, enthused, effective, and excited about ways to MOVE with passion, purpose, and intention by inviting Bridgette L. Collins to speak at your event.

Contact her today:

www.NextLevelHRSolutions.com

(972) 768-3488

Your Under-Construction Worksheets

WORKSHEET

FAMILY

GOAL: To have healthy family relationships.

Plan/Act

SELF-ANALYSIS

What do I need to do to become a better version of myself? Why? Benefits?

_____

_____

_____

_____

_____

_____

_____

_____

_____

_____

_____

_____

_____

ACTIVITY 1:

_____

_____

_____

_____

_____

ACTIVITY 2:

_____

_____

_____

_____

_____

ACTIVITY 3:

_____

_____

_____

_____

_____

SELF-TRANSFORMATION

What do I need to do to get into alignment with who I am, who I want to be, and what I'm trying to do in my life? (e.g., shift in perspective, thoughts, feelings, and actions) Why? Benefits?

_____

_____

_____

_____

_____

_____

_____

_____

_____

_____

_____

_____

_____

_____

_____

ACTIVITY 1:

_____

_____

_____

_____

_____

ACTIVITY 2:

_____

_____

_____

_____

_____

ACTIVITY 3:

_____

_____

_____

_____

_____

SELF-EVOLUTION

What sources (e.g., coach, mentor, etc.) and resources (e.g., books, webinars, etc.) do I need to evolve in my life? Why? Benefits?

_____

_____

_____

_____

_____

_____

_____

_____

_____

_____

_____

_____

_____

_____

_____

ACTIVITY 1:

_____

_____

_____

_____

_____

ACTIVITY 2:

_____

_____

_____

_____

_____

ACTIVITY 3:

_____

_____

_____

_____

_____

SELF-NARRATION

What/who do I need to incorporate to live the legacy I want to leave? Why? Benefits?

_____

_____

_____

_____

_____

_____

_____

_____

_____

_____

_____

_____

_____

_____

_____

ACTIVITY 1:

_____

_____

_____

_____

_____

ACTIVITY 2:

_____

_____

_____

_____

_____

ACTIVITY 3:

_____

_____

_____

_____

_____

DESIRED OUTCOME

WORKSHEET

FRIENDS

GOAL: To have a trusted circle of friends.

Plan/Act

SELF-ANALYSIS

What do I need to do to become a better version of myself? Why? Benefits?

_____

_____

_____

_____

_____

_____

_____

_____

_____

_____

_____

_____

ACTIVITY 1:

_____

_____

_____

_____

_____

ACTIVITY 2:

_____

_____

_____

_____

_____

ACTIVITY 3:

_____

_____

_____

_____

_____

SELF-TRANSFORMATION

What do I need to do to get into alignment with who I am, who I want to be, and what I'm trying to do in my life? (e.g., shift in perspective, thoughts, feelings, and actions) Why? Benefits?

_____

_____

_____

_____

_____

_____

_____

_____

_____

_____

_____

_____

_____

_____

_____

_____

ACTIVITY 1:

_____

_____

_____

_____

_____

ACTIVITY 2:

_____

_____

_____

_____

_____

ACTIVITY 3:

_____

_____

_____

_____

_____

SELF-EVOLUTION

What sources (e.g., coach, mentor, etc.) and resources (e.g., books, webinars, etc.) do I need to evolve in my life? Why? Benefits?

_____

_____

_____

_____

_____

_____

_____

_____

_____

_____

_____

_____

_____

_____

ACTIVITY 1:

_____

_____

_____

_____

_____

ACTIVITY 2:

_____

_____

_____

_____

_____

ACTIVITY 3:

_____

_____

_____

_____

_____

SELF-NARRATION

What/who do I need to incorporate to live the legacy I want to leave? Why? Benefits?

_____

_____

_____

_____

_____

_____

_____

_____

_____

_____

_____

_____

_____

_____

_____

_____

_____

ACTIVITY 1:

_____

_____

_____

_____

_____

ACTIVITY 2:

_____

_____

_____

_____

_____

ACTIVITY 3:

_____

_____

_____

_____

_____

DESIRED OUTCOME

WORKSHEET

FINANCES

GOAL: To be financially secure.

Plan/Act

SELF-ANALYSIS

What do I need to do to become a better version of myself? Why? Benefits?

_____

_____

_____

_____

_____

_____

_____

_____

_____

_____

_____

ACTIVITY 1:

_____

_____

_____

_____

_____

ACTIVITY 2:

_____

_____

_____

_____

_____

ACTIVITY 3:

_____

_____

_____

_____

_____

SELF-TRANSFORMATION

What do I need to do to get into alignment with who I am, who I want to be, and what I'm trying to do in my life? (e.g., shift in perspective, thoughts, feelings, and actions) Why? Benefits?

_____

_____

_____

_____

_____

_____

_____

_____

_____

_____

_____

_____

_____

_____

ACTIVITY 1:

_____

_____

_____

_____

_____

ACTIVITY 2:

_____

_____

_____

_____

_____

ACTIVITY 3:

_____

_____

_____

_____

_____

SELF-EVOLUTION

What sources (e.g., coach, mentor, etc.) and resources (e.g., books, webinars, etc.) do I need to evolve in my life? Why? Benefits?

_____

_____

_____

_____

_____

_____

_____

_____

_____

_____

_____

_____

_____

_____

_____

ACTIVITY 1:

_____

_____

_____

_____

_____

ACTIVITY 2:

_____

_____

_____

_____

_____

ACTIVITY 3:

_____

_____

_____

_____

_____

SELF-NARRATION

What/who do I need to incorporate to live the legacy I want to leave? Why? Benefits?

_____

_____

_____

_____

_____

_____

_____

_____

_____

_____

_____

_____

_____

_____

_____

_____

ACTIVITY 1:

_____

_____

_____

_____

_____

ACTIVITY 2:

_____

_____

_____

_____

_____

ACTIVITY 3:

_____

_____

_____

_____

_____

SAMPLE MONTHLY BUDGET

Monthly Income		
Item	Hypothetical Amount	Write In Your Amount
Income 1	$3,000.00	
Income 2	$1,000.00	
Other	$250.00	
Total Income	**$4,250.00**	
Monthly Expenses		
Rent/Mortgage	$1,150.00	
Electric	$120.00	
Gas	$40.00	
Water/Trash	$75.00	
Cell Phone	$85.00	
Groceries	$350.00	
Car Payment	$466.00	
Auto Expenses	$140.00	
Student Loans	$150.00	
Credit Cards	$325.00	
Auto Insurance	$88.00	
Personal Care	$135.00	
Cable/Streaming/Internet Services	$150.00	
Entertainment	$200.00	
Miscellaneous	$100.00	
Total Expenses	**$3,574.00**	
"Under Construction" Leftover	**$676.00**	

DESIRED OUTCOME

WORKSHEET

HEALTH/FITNESS

GOAL: To achieve and maintain good health.

Plan/Act

SELF-ANALYSIS

What do I need to do to become a better version of myself? Why? Benefits?

_____

_____

_____

_____

_____

_____

_____

_____

_____

_____

_____

_____

ACTIVITY 1:

_____

_____

_____

_____

_____

ACTIVITY 2:

_____

_____

_____

_____

_____

ACTIVITY 3:

_____

_____

_____

_____

_____

SELF-TRANSFORMATION

What do I need to do to get into alignment with who I am, who I want to be, and what I'm trying to do in my life? (e.g., shift in perspective, thoughts, feelings, and actions) Why? Benefits?

_____

_____

_____

_____

_____

_____

_____

_____

_____

_____

_____

_____

_____

_____

_____

ACTIVITY 1:

_____

_____

_____

_____

_____

ACTIVITY 2:

_____

_____

_____

_____

_____

ACTIVITY 3:

_____

_____

_____

_____

_____

SELF-EVOLUTION

What sources (e.g., coach, mentor, etc.) and resources (e.g., books, webinars, etc.) do I need to evolve in my life? Why? Benefits?

_____

_____

_____

_____

_____

_____

_____

_____

_____

_____

_____

_____

_____

_____

_____

_____

_____

ACTIVITY 1:

_____

_____

_____

_____

_____

ACTIVITY 2:

_____

_____

_____

_____

_____

ACTIVITY 3:

_____

_____

_____

_____

_____

SELF-NARRATION

What/who do I need to incorporate to live the legacy I want to leave? Why? Benefits?

_____

_____

_____

_____

_____

_____

_____

_____

_____

_____

_____

_____

_____

_____

_____

_____

ACTIVITY 1:

_____

_____

_____

_____

_____

ACTIVITY 2:

_____

_____

_____

_____

_____

ACTIVITY 3:

_____

_____

_____

_____

_____

DESIRED OUTCOME

WORKSHEET

CAREER/BUSINESS

GOAL: To flourish in my professional endeavors.

Plan/Act

SELF-ANALYSIS

What do I need to do to become a better version of myself? Why? Benefits?

_____

_____

_____

_____

_____

_____

_____

_____

_____

_____

_____

_____

ACTIVITY 1:

_____

_____

_____

_____

_____

ACTIVITY 2:

_____

_____

_____

_____

_____

ACTIVITY 3:

_____

_____

_____

_____

_____

SELF-TRANSFORMATION

What do I need to do to get into alignment with who I am, who I want to be, and what I'm trying to do in my life? (e.g., shift in perspective, thoughts, feelings, and actions) Why? Benefits?

_____

_____

_____

_____

_____

_____

_____

_____

_____

_____

_____

_____

_____

_____

_____

_____

ACTIVITY 1:

_____

_____

_____

_____

_____

ACTIVITY 2:

_____

_____

_____

_____

_____

ACTIVITY 3:

_____

_____

_____

_____

_____

SELF-EVOLUTION

What sources (e.g., coach, mentor, etc.) and resources (e.g., books, webinars, etc.) do I need to evolve in my life? Why? Benefits?

_____

_____

_____

_____

_____

_____

_____

_____

_____

_____

_____

_____

_____

_____

_____

_____

ACTIVITY 1:

_____

_____

_____

_____

_____

ACTIVITY 2:

_____

_____

_____

_____

_____

ACTIVITY 3:

_____

_____

_____

_____

_____

SELF-NARRATION

What/who do I need to incorporate to live the legacy I want to leave? Why? Benefits?

_____

_____

_____

_____

_____

_____

_____

_____

_____

_____

_____

_____

_____

_____

_____

ACTIVITY 1:

_____

_____

_____

_____

_____

ACTIVITY 2:

_____

_____

_____

_____

_____

ACTIVITY 3:

_____

_____

_____

_____

_____

DESIRED OUTCOME

WORKSHEET

COMMUNITY

GOAL: To be involved in community events.

Plan/Act

<u>**SELF-ANALYSIS**</u>

What do I need to do to become a better version of myself? Why? Benefits?

_____

_____

_____

_____

_____

_____

_____

_____

_____

_____

_____

ACTIVITY 1:

_____

_____

_____

_____

_____

ACTIVITY 2:

_____

_____

_____

_____

_____

ACTIVITY 3:

_____

_____

_____

_____

_____

SELF-TRANSFORMATION

What do I need to do to get into alignment with who I am, who I want to be, and what I'm trying to do in my life? (e.g., shift in perspective, thoughts, feelings, and actions) Why? Benefits?

ACTIVITY 1:

_____

_____

_____

_____

_____

ACTIVITY 2:

_____

_____

_____

_____

_____

ACTIVITY 3:

_____

_____

_____

_____

_____

SELF-EVOLUTION

What sources (e.g., coach, mentor, etc.) and resources (e.g., books, webinars, etc.) do I need to evolve in my life? Why? Benefits?

ACTIVITY 1:

_____

_____

_____

_____

_____

ACTIVITY 2:

_____

_____

_____

_____

_____

ACTIVITY 3:

_____

_____

_____

_____

_____

SELF-NARRATION

What/who do I need to incorporate to live the legacy I want to leave? Why? Benefits?

_____

_____

_____

_____

_____

_____

_____

_____

_____

_____

_____

_____

_____

_____

_____

_____

ACTIVITY 1:

_____

_____

_____

_____

_____

ACTIVITY 2:

_____

_____

_____

_____

_____

ACTIVITY 3:

_____

_____

_____

_____

_____

DESIRED OUTCOME

WORKSHEET

FUN/LEISURE

GOAL: To be active physically and socially.

Plan/Act

SELF-ANALYSIS

What do I need to do to become a better version of myself? Why? Benefits?

_____

_____

_____

_____

_____

_____

_____

_____

_____

_____

ACTIVITY 1:

_____

_____

_____

_____

_____

ACTIVITY 2:

_____

_____

_____

_____

_____

ACTIVITY 3:

_____

_____

_____

_____

_____

SELF-TRANSFORMATION

What do I need to do to get into alignment with who I am, who I want to be, and what I'm trying to do in my life? (e.g., shift in perspective, thoughts, feelings, and actions) Why? Benefits?

_____

_____

_____

_____

_____

_____

_____

_____

_____

_____

_____

_____

_____

_____

_____

_____

ACTIVITY 1:

_____

_____

_____

_____

_____

ACTIVITY 2:

_____

_____

_____

_____

_____

ACTIVITY 3:

_____

_____

_____

_____

_____

SELF-EVOLUTION

What sources (e.g., coach, mentor, etc.) and resources (e.g., books, webinars, etc.) do I need to evolve in my life? Why? Benefits?

_____

_____

_____

_____

_____

_____

_____

_____

_____

_____

_____

_____

_____

_____

_____

ACTIVITY 1:

_____

_____

_____

_____

_____

ACTIVITY 2:

_____

_____

_____

_____

_____

ACTIVITY 3:

_____

_____

_____

_____

_____

SELF-NARRATION

What/who do I need to incorporate to live the legacy I want to leave? Why? Benefits?

_____

_____

_____

_____

_____

_____

_____

_____

_____

_____

_____

_____

_____

_____

_____

_____

ACTIVITY 1:

_____

_____

_____

_____

_____

ACTIVITY 2:

_____

_____

_____

_____

_____

ACTIVITY 3:

_____

_____

_____

_____

_____

DESIRED OUTCOME

WORKSHEET

ATTITUDINAL

GOAL: To have a positive attitude.

Plan/Act

SELF-ANALYSIS

What do I need to do to become a better version of myself? Why? Benefits?

_____

_____

_____

_____

_____

_____

_____

_____

_____

_____

ACTIVITY 1:

_____

_____

_____

_____

_____

ACTIVITY 2:

_____

_____

_____

_____

_____

ACTIVITY 3:

_____

_____

_____

_____

_____

SELF-TRANSFORMATION

What do I need to do to get into alignment with who I am, who I want to be, and what I'm trying to do in my life? (e.g., shift in perspective, thoughts, feelings, and actions) Why? Benefits?

_____

_____

_____

_____

_____

_____

_____

_____

_____

_____

_____

_____

_____

ACTIVITY 1:

_____

_____

_____

_____

_____

ACTIVITY 2:

_____

_____

_____

_____

_____

ACTIVITY 3:

_____

_____

_____

_____

_____

SELF-EVOLUTION

What sources (e.g., coach, mentor, etc.) and resources (e.g., books, webinars, etc.) do I need to evolve in my life? Why? Benefits?

_____

_____

_____

_____

_____

_____

_____

_____

_____

_____

_____

_____

_____

_____

_____

ACTIVITY 1:

_____

_____

_____

_____

_____

ACTIVITY 2:

_____

_____

_____

_____

_____

ACTIVITY 3:

_____

_____

_____

_____

_____

SELF-NARRATION

What/who do I need to incorporate to live the legacy I want to leave? Why? Benefits?

_____

_____

_____

_____

_____

_____

_____

_____

_____

_____

_____

_____

_____

_____

_____

_____

ACTIVITY 1:

_____

_____

_____

_____

_____

ACTIVITY 2:

_____

_____

_____

_____

_____

ACTIVITY 3:

_____

_____

_____

_____

_____

DESIRED OUTCOME

ACKNOWLEDGMENTS

I am so grateful to the contributions of my FAV Five Roadrunners to this book. For years they've been a blessing to me, and now, they've been a blessing to you too!

Ken Johnson

Ken, a lifelong runner and a legend in the East Texas community, has completed more than 1,200 races, including 101 full or ultra-marathons, and 106 half-marathons. In the early '90s, he wrote a book, *How to Put On a Road Race.* In 1985, he co-founded the Seven Hills Running Club, which is still active today, thirty-six years later. He wrote a running column for the *Huntsville Item* newspaper for ten years. Ken is a streak runner and has only missed thirty-one days of running since 1997. You can keep up with Ken at https://kenstreaker.blogspot.com.

Joyce Johnson

Joyce started her sales career in the professional sports industry and later entered the telecommunications industry, leading to a role as sales director in global markets and worked during deregulation of both the telecommunications and energy markets. She spent the past two years growing the Why Sales Network brand after a twenty-year career as a sales leader, earning top recognition as #1 seller in 2017 and 2018. Why Sales Network is a global sales training organization dedicated to empowering the next generation of business leaders.

For over fifteen years, Joyce has had the opportunity to mentor a group of her favorite "college students." As she listened to their experiences and witnessed them take leaps of faith on their pathway to the workforce, she was inspired to create a platform to assist them in their development by creating Why Sales Network Student Foundation. Learn more about Joyce at http://www.iamjoycejohnson.com.

Daniel Henderson

Since 2007, Daniel has been a leading estate agent in Texas. He recognizes and values the trust his clients place in him and strives with each given opportunity to ensure they have an exceptional buying or purchasing experience. In 2018, Daniel became the co-owner of OTR Masters Trucking, LLC. He and his partner purchased their first truck, acquired a contract with one of the largest and most trusted Global shipping companies, and started moving freight throughout the US. In the midst of his endeavors, Daniel has worked twenty-three years for AT&T.

Liletta Harlem

Liletta is the author of *Celebrating A Legacy of Courage and Resolve*, and *I Can Fix My...* She is an event coordinator, motivational speaker, and women's group facilitator for domestic violence. She is also the host and producer of the YouTube Series, *Pivotal Moments with Liletta*, and CEO and founder of her company, My Natural Me, which focuses on empowering and uplifting women. Learn more about Liletta at http://www.lilettaharlem.com/.

Anthony Reed

Anthony is the co-founder of the National Black Marathoners Association (NBMA), which is the nation's largest not-for-profit organization promoting distance running in the Black community. He is also the CEO of the Caribbean Endurance Sports Corporation and organizer of the Five-Island Challenge marathon and half-marathon. He is one of about fifty people in the world who has completed the marathon "hat trick." This involves finishing (1) at least one hundred marathons, (2) in all fifty States, and (3) all seven continents. He won age group and weight division medals and trophies for placing in national and international 5Ks, marathons (26.2 miles/42.2K), and biathlons (biking/running). He's also a triathlete and the first Black person in the world to complete marathons on all seven continents, including Antarctica. He is also the author of *Running Shoes Are Cheaper than Insulin: Marathon Adventures on All Seven Continents* and *From the Road Race to the Rat Race: Essays from a Black Executive Marathoner*. He produced and directed the 2021 documentary, *Breaking Three Hours: Trailblazing African American Women Marathoners,* about nine National Black Distance Running Hall of Fame inductees who broke three hours in the marathon. Learn more about Anthony Reed at http://www.reed-cpa.com/ and http://www.runningtoleadership.com/.

ABOUT THE AUTHOR

Bridgette L. Collins is the owner of Next Level HR Solutions. In addition to serving as a business partner to public and private sector employers in the areas of HR compliance, employee relations, management/employee development, and performance management, Bridgette works with clients on establishing workplace health and fitness promotions.

Bridgette is the author of three books, *Broken in Plain Sight*, *Destined to Live Healthier: Mind, Body, and Soul*, and *Imagine Living Healthier: Mind, Body, and Soul*. She is featured in *The Ultimate Runner* by Ultimate HCI Books, publisher of the *Chicken Soup for the Soul* series. Her story, "Never Give Up: My Journey to Become a Runner," of transitioning from the sofa to the streets to become a marathon runner has inspired many to use running as their fitness option to get fit and stay fit.

When she is not performing one of her human resources consulting services or not writing at her favorite restaurant spot, Bridgette spends most of time reading, cooking, working out at LA Fitness, and training for her next race event. A true sports fanatic, she enjoys watching the various NFL football games on Monday and Thursday nights, and all day on Sundays, and the various NBA basketball games throughout the week on ESPN and TNT.

Keep in touch with Bridgette via the web:

Website: https://nextlevelhrsolutions.com/

Facebook: https://www.facebook.com/askcoachcollins

Twitter: https://twitter.com/askcoachcollins

Instagram: https://www.instagram.com/bridgettelcollins/